Coaching *and* *Mentoring*

AN INTRODUCTORY GUIDE FOR CHRISTIANS

ANDY PECK

Copyright © CWR 2014

Published by CWR, Waverley Abbey House, Waverley Lane,
Farnham, Surrey GU9 8EP, UK. CWR is a Registered Charity
– Number 294387 and a Limited Company registered in England –
Registration Number 1990308.

For a list of National Distributors visit www.cwr.org.uk/distributors
Unless otherwise indicated, all Scripture references are from the
Holy Bible: New International Version (NIV), copyright © 1973, 1978,
1984, 2011 by Biblica (formerly the International Bible Society).
Concept development, editing, design and production by CWR.
Printed in the UK by Page Bros.
ISBN: 978-1-78259-271-6

Acknowledgements

My thanks to Bev Shepherd, who is a colleague on the Coaching and Mentoring course. She read the first draft, and made some helpful comments and suggestions. She is mentioned in the book on a few occasions as 'my colleague, Bev'. I am very grateful for help and ongoing inspiration in this field.

Some of the material on mentoring was taken from a course led by a former colleague, Ron Kallmier. I am grateful to him for that excellent course.

My thanks too to all those who have attended the coaching and mentoring courses at CWR. Their feedback has helped improve the course, and this book too.

Contents

Preface

CWR has conducted a number of courses on coaching and mentoring in the last decade; one-day courses such as Coaching Others, Mentoring Others, two-day courses including Introduction to Biblical Coaching, Intermediate Course in Biblical Coaching, and a three-day course called Coaching and Mentoring. This book aims to distil some of the foundational material that has shaped those courses.

I lead the three-day Coaching and Mentoring course with Bev Shepherd, who works as a full-time coach and mentor. Some of the coaching material has been taken from the parts of the course she led. It is an introductory book aimed at those who have a vague idea of the topic, and would like to reflect on what coaching and mentoring are, and how they may use the skills that have developed with these disciplines within their daily life, working life, or supported or volunteer ministry. Some may discover that they want go on to make a part-time or full-time living as a coach or mentor.

We will look at the two topics together in the first chapter, before looking first at coaching, then mentoring, separately. A concluding chapter looks at some steps you may want to take after completing the book. Some use both coaching and mentoring in their work, others find that they are more suited to one than the other. If you think that you have an initial preference, it would still be worth reading about the other discipline, if only to help those you coach and mentor to better understand what you are and aren't doing.

It is a book for Christians who attend and benefit from local churches and have a heart to see God's people flourish where He has placed them. Coaching and mentoring are increasingly seen as a normal part of local church life; a few churches have made coaches and mentors available to those who attend, some use mentoring and coaching as tools for spiritual growth in lieu of a small group network. Many church leaders see a coach or mentor as part of their ongoing ministry. My prayer is that this book will aid the use of these key disciplines in the church's life and witness so that the church may be all that it can and should be as the twenty-first century witness for Christ in the UK and overseas.

Introduction to coaching and mentoring

Throughout the history of the Church, Christians have helped one another through one-to-one conversations. You have probably benefited from this yourself.

In recent decades, many Christians have found that the specific tools provided by the disciplines of coaching and mentoring have given fresh insights and approaches to enable them to be effective in their help.

But what can be very confusing in these fields is that there is no universal definition of the two terms. I have known Christians talk enthusiastically about their mentoring experience. When they describe what they do, they are describing what others would insist is coaching. Every course at CWR includes a clear description of the course content, but we have attendees of coaching and mentoring courses who are surprised with the material covered.

In this book we see the main distinction between the two activities like this:

A coach seeks to facilitate the growth and progress in someone through non-directive conversation.
A mentor aids growth through directive conversation based on their own experience and skill.

You will note that the key distinguishing words in this definition are 'non-directive' and 'directive'.

In non-directive conversation, a coach aims to help the coachee reflect on their life and possible solutions to whatever it is they are focusing on. They do this through listening and questioning, which helps to open up the topic. The coachee would typically do 80 per cent of the talking.

A mentor would expect to do more talking as they are more directive in the way they share their wisdom on the area in which they are mentoring.

A coach may have little or no direct awareness of the discipline or area in which the coachee is engaged. A mentor, under this definition, is experienced in the area in which they are mentoring. Indeed, the mentor is specifically chosen for their capacity to impart their skill and experience to the person they seek to help.

A coach would rarely say, 'do it this way', whereas a mentor might often suggest that the mentoree imitate their practice, especially if they are concerned with a particular area of expertise.

In our experience Christians typically find the mentoring approach easier to grasp, especially if they are in Christian leadership. This is because Christians are used to being directed from a pulpit, or, in a leadership context, through instruction based on the Bible to which they must submit. It is easy for them to understand that there might be experienced Christians who might be able to mentor them in an area of their Christian life. They find it harder to grasp that the non-directive methods used by a coach might also be valuable. We will look later at the rationale from a biblical perspective and also note that good mentoring, as defined above, can use non-directive approaches too.

Having made the distinction between coaching and mentoring, let it be said that there is some fluidity in practice. What matters is that the person is being helped in their growth, whatever area that is, and the wise coach and/or mentor uses all the tools at their disposal. You may believe you are especially equipped to coach, to mentor, or to do both.

As we have hinted, when talking about coaching and mentoring, you need to be clear on the distinction between the two, and check that those you work with understand how the words 'coaching' and 'mentoring' are being used.

We use this definition of mentor, in part, because the word 'mentor' comes from Greek mythology and suggests this kind of approach. Mentes was the son of Alcumus, and a friend of Odysseus. When Odysseus left for the Trojan War, he placed Mentes in charge of his son, Telemachus, to help bring him up. Of course, some of Mentes' work might have been non-directive, but the role of a pseudo-parent is to be prescriptive and directional as they impart wisdom and skills into a young life.

Professional bodies reflect this lack of a universal definition. The Chartered Institute of Personnel and Development (CIPD) fact sheet on coaching and mentoring admits the confusion about definitions but adds this: 'Some see coaching as conversations which involve non-directive facilitation, whereas mentoring has a higher direction component connected to the experience of the person mentoring.'

If you study the disciplines at Oxford Brookes University you will be told:

> Coaching and mentoring are both human development processes that involve structured, focused interaction and the use of appropriate strategies, tools and techniques to promote desirable and sustainable change for the benefit of the client and other stakeholders. The main distinction between the two terms is that coaching does not rely necessarily on the specific experience and knowledge of the coach being greater than that of the client. We believe that mentoring is enhanced by the use of coaching methods, but that it also allows knowledge and experience to be conveyed to the client.[1]

The Chartered Institute of Personnel and Development goes on to highlight activities that are common to both coaching and mentoring.

Coaching and mentoring:
1. Facilitate the exploration of needs, motivations, desires, skills and thought processes to assist the individual in making real, lasting change.
2. Use questioning techniques to facilitate a client's own thought processes in order to identify solutions and actions.
3. Support the client in setting appropriate goals and methods of assessing progress in relation to these goals.
4. Observe, listen and ask questions to understand the client's situation
5. Encourage a commitment to action and the development of lasting personal growth and change.
6. Ensure that clients develop personal competencies and do not develop unhealthy dependencies on the coaching or mentoring relationship.

(Adapted from list at: www.coachingnetwork.org.uk)

We will look at coaching and mentoring in separate sections of this book, but you will note that there is some overlap in the two.

Coaching and mentoring in a Christian context

The activity of coaching and mentoring meshes with a biblical outlook on life. The words are not specifically mentioned but there are themes within Scripture which make them activities that tie in well with what a Christ follower is looking to do.

1. God made us for relationship with Himself and others

Adam and Eve were created for relationship with God and enjoyed communion with Him. We believe that these early chapters of Genesis provide a foundation to our understanding of how God intends human beings to relate to Him. We are told in Genesis 1:26–27 that we are made 'in the image of God'. This phrase has been variously understood but probably conveys the idea that we share some of God's essential characteristics: that we are relational, rational, volitional, personal, spiritual, emotional beings. So we have a godly instinct to relate to others, including for many, a lifelong partner, but also a host of other meaningful relationships.

Of course, this relationship with God was fractured when Adam and Eve rebelled against God. In due course when God sets about rescuing humanity from its rebellion He chooses to work in the family of Abraham and his descendants, and through the nation of Israel. This would become a model community, demonstrating what God is like to the world around. His work and powerful involvement was a sign that He really could be trusted.

When Jesus comes as the Saviour and Lord of Israel, and the rest of the world, He too builds a community of followers whom He would train to carry on the work of telling the world of His love and goodness. The book of Acts records the way in which believers who acknowledged Jesus as Lord formed communities across the Roman Empire and beyond, as the message of God's love spread in the early decades after Christ's death, resurrection and ascension.

Relationships are a key part of God's purposes for us all. We are made to 'know and be known'. Good coaching and mentoring develops intentional relationships and therefore a context for truth to be shared and actions taken.

2. God made us to take action (Gen. 1:26–28)

Coaching and mentoring encourage people to address issues and deal with them. Throughout Scripture, God is urging people to do just that.

In Genesis 1:26–28 we read:

> Then God said, 'Let us make mankind in our image, in our likeness, so that they may rule over the fish in the sea and the birds in the sky, over the livestock and all the wild animals, and over all the creatures that move along the ground.' So God created mankind in his own image, in the image of God he created them; male and female he created them. God blessed them and said to them, 'Be fruitful and increase in number; fill the earth and subdue it. Rule over the fish in the sea and the birds in the sky and over every living creature that moves on the ground.'

Having dominion over the likes of cats, dogs and guinea pigs may not seem a big deal, but the implications of the above passage are more far reaching than you may have realised. What does it mean to 'fill the earth and subdue it?' Clearly there was something about planet Earth that required human intervention under God, even at the beginning! Scholar G.K. Beale has conducted an intensive study of the passage and sees a similarity between the Genesis account and the way peoples in the ancient Near East described the building of a temple, and placing a priest as an 'image bearer of the king' in the heart of it. He argues that: 'This meant the presence of God, which was initially to be limited to the temple of Eden and the adjoining garden, was to be extended throughout the whole earth by his image bearers, as they themselves represented and reflected his glorious presence and attributes' ('Garden Temple', article by G. K. Beale, www.kerux.com/doc/1802A1.asp).

If you think we are a little off-track from our topic, let me reassure you. Coaching and mentoring can be used for many purposes, but Christians are enabled to connect people with the overall narrative of what God is doing in this world. They have a capacity, under God, to take authority over the world which they love in Christ's name. They support people so they can be all that God intends. It can give people a sense of purpose as they realise that their life is part of something bigger – that God purposes that they play a real and valuable part in an eternal project that sweeps down through time, through their life and beyond.

3. We all face hindrances in being the people God intends us to be

As Christians we know that we are infected by the sin virus that affects our relationship with God, with ourselves, with those close to us and with the world in which we live.

The Genesis account tells us how Satan was given authority when Adam and Eve sinned and trusted the lie of the serpent rather than the word of God.

Without the belief that God takes care of us, we naturally turn in on ourselves and are naturally consumed with looking after 'number one'.

Both coaching and mentoring help us step out from under the oppression we feel, caused by, as John puts it, by 'the world, the flesh and the devil' (paraphrased from 1 John 2:16) and instead walk in the goodness of the purposes that God has for us.

4. Christ's life, death and resurrection are central to who we are as believers

Christians use coaching and mentoring within the context of the grace of God seen in Christ. As Christians we centre our understanding of life in Christ. He lived the perfect life, died on behalf of us sinners and rose again as the Lord of all, able to give salvation to all who put their confidence in Him. Christians rest in His finished work and seek to follow Him as their Lord.

This is an important foundation. Outside the Christian context, coaching and mentoring can be used to help people pursue goals and ambitions that are essentially self-focused. People are told that good coaching and mentoring can 'help you achieve your dreams', whatever they may be. Christian coaching and mentoring urges a Christ-focused approach while being sensitive to where people are in their journey as we trust the Holy Spirit to guide us all towards greater trust in Him.

5. God gives us authority

The Genesis account of creation tells us that the devil had no authority over us until it was given to him. Interestingly, after Jesus rose from the dead He tells His followers that: 'All authority in heaven and on earth has been given to me. Therefore go and make disciples of all nations' (Matt. 28:18–19). It wasn't that God was somehow unable to work because of Satan – that would be absurd. The whole Old Testament underlines the working out of

God's purposes. But there was a sense in which Jesus gives a new authority to all who follow Him. The Twelve had glimpses of that when they were commissioned by Jesus to heal the sick, cast out demons and raise the dead. They saw the signs of the kingdom that they had experienced when Jesus was physically on earth, and also after Jesus had ascended.

You will never coach or mentor anyone who is not affected and marred by sin. Equally you can know that everyone you work with is loved by God, precious to Him and will know God's rich involvement in their lives as they welcome Him to guide and direct them.

Armed with these perspectives, coaching and mentoring can help Christians in many areas. We might list the following:

Walking with God

The New Testament describes the battle every believer faces. Even when we know who we are in Christ, we have a daily battle to stay close to Christ. We know we are to love God and love our neighbour, but our heart is drawn too often to look after ourselves. Coaching and mentoring helps us get up close and personal about the daily struggle and find ways to overcome sin and choose righteousness through one to one conversations that help us be accountable to someone else for the work we do.

Walking with others

As the ditty goes, 'To dwell above with the saints we love will be grace and glory, but to live below with the saints we know, that's a different story.'

The Church is a company of imperfect people and it's no surprise that we will have difficulties from time to time. Disagreements should be dealt with one on one as encouraged by Jesus, and in most cases coaches and mentors would not expect to be involved. But when there are ongoing patterns of behaviour that impact others, good coaching and mentoring helps people understand where they struggle, why they struggle, and through prayer and wise practice, develop new ways of living.

Tony Stoltzfus, a coach in the US, puts it this way in his book, *Leadership Coaching*:

> People do not feel truly believed in until they are truly known
> … I believe the biggest reason Christians in general experience
> so little transformation in their lives is that they ignore the

Bible's relational mandate for how to affect change. We were never meant to live the Christian life alone. Christianity is an interdependent community-oriented faith. And yet, when we set out to improve our prayer life, or deal with an anger problem, or become a better father; most of the time we work on it completely alone. Coaching puts change back into the context of a learning community, where God always intended for it to be.[2]

Taking leadership

God has made us all with a capacity to lead, if only our own lives or those of our immediate family. You will discover later that coaching and mentoring help us imagine and dream about a better future for ourselves and our world. Christians know that God gives them hope and a future but often need help taking action to implement initiatives in keeping with that future. If that future seems scary for you, coaching and mentoring can help you explore why that is. Sometimes past disappointments have not only made us fearful of 'building up our hopes' in case we are let down, but may also have led to negative beliefs about the future. My colleague, Bev Shepherd, has come across various of these beliefs in her work as a coach, including: 'things always get worse', 'something is bound to go wrong' and 'I'm too old to start this now'. Helping people hear God's truth instead of their self-realising negative beliefs may move us more towards spiritual direction than pure coaching, yet can be vital in helping people grow.

Building teams

I host a radio show on leadership with Premier Radio and find that church leaders often struggle to attract and mobilise volunteers to their work. Coaching and mentoring programmes provide a context for gift discovery and a means of helping volunteers be effective in their service.

Improving service

Coaching and mentoring help us improve how we serve God: discovering and utilising gifts and honing those we have. We are often ignorant of our true contribution or how we might take things up a notch. Someone skilled in our field can assist us through mentoring. A good coach can guide our self understanding so we appreciate how we might serve God.

Coaching, mentoring and other one to one methods in a Christian context

We are often asked how coaching and mentoring sits alongside other types of one to one intervention. The following list helps to distinguish the kinds of help that may be offered.

Helping process	**What this means in practice**
Coaching	One person facilitates another to learn and change within a biblical framework. The coach helps the coachee to develop their potential towards Christian maturity.
Mentoring	Someone more experienced in the faith imparts skills and knowledge of walking with God to a less experienced person.
Counselling	A counsellor enables the counsellee to develop a healing and empowering relationship with God and see His perspective on specific personal problems.
Pastoral care	The carer looks after the general personal, spiritual and social wellbeing of another within a biblical framework.
Spiritual direction	A director journeys with another to enable them to cultivate a deeper personal relationship with God. Prayer and conversation are directed towards deepening intimacy with God and greater surrender to Him.
Discipleship	Someone who is committed to following Jesus helps another believer to know and practise the teaching of Jesus. They may use coaching or mentoring as part of their help.
Consulting	A consultant imparts their wisdom, knowledge and perspective to a person or group's situation.

It is clear that there is some overlap between some of the disciplines and coaching and mentoring. If you work in a pastoral context, you may find that you need to coach or mentor the person you visit, or pass them on to someone who can. I once helped lead a spiritual direction week at CWR, during which, one of my co-leaders remarked on the similarity between some of the spiritual direction approaches and coaching. In the latter stages of counselling, when the person you are helping has seen a degree of improvement, coaching can be used to help them look forward into the future.

Mentoring has a strong overlap with teaching. You might choose to teach someone by sharing their skills and wisdom and modelling the activity.

Counselling and coaching/mentoring

We can note the difference between counselling, mentoring and coaching as follows:

COUNSELLING					OK			COACHING/MENTORING		
-10	-8	-6	-4	-2	0	2	4	6	8	10

-10 to 0 = troubled areas that need help
0 = 'normal': healthy but no progress
0 to 10 = growing 'fulfilment' in Christ

This scale reminds us that counselling typically helps people who are troubled. Coaching and mentoring helps people who are basically 'OK' but look to make progress.

In practice it can be hard at times to differentiate between a situation or issue that needs counselling and one that needs mentoring and coaching. If a person seems unwilling to overcome crippling poor self-esteem, do they need someone to work on poor self-talk through counselling? Or do they need support to take appropriate action that will improve their self-esteem?

There is some overlap in the ways in which someone will be helped. A good counsellor will look to a coaching or mentoring approach as the person recovers and becomes focused on the future.

Coaching and mentoring and you

You are reading this because you have some interest in using the principles of coaching and mentoring in your own life. So at the very start it will be useful to do some preliminary thinking on what you might bring to your work. As you read this book you will be able to clarify, underline or adjust your thinking.

Coaching and mentoring in a Christian context is a relationship between three persons (the coachee, the coach and the Holy Spirit; the mentor, mentoree and the Holy Spirit) with specific Christ-honouring aims and within a biblical framework of spiritual growth.

What you bring as a coach and mentor is unique – your background, experience, values, beliefs and gifts. It is therefore key that you reflect on what you may bring to the relationship.

Fill in the grid on the next page according to these descriptions:

Background
Reflect on what makes you who you are, including where you are from, your family, your personality and your expectations growing up.

Experience
If you were writing a script of the movie of your life, what would be the main events you would include? What makes you laugh and cry? Have there been times of extreme emotion? Any key turning points?

Relationship with God
When did this begin? How? Has it been a settled relationship? What have been the major faith spurts? Have there been disappointments? Where are things now? Where would you like them to be?

Giftings
Include here your talents and aptitudes as well as the gifts God has given you to serve Him. What have you done that others have affirmed as being God at work in and through you? You may want to ask a friend what they think you bring.

Values
What are some of the core values that you live your life by? You might call them 'maxims', such as 'people matter', 'work before play', 'always have fun' ,'think of those less fortunate than me', 'don't waste time'.

Beliefs about people and how they change

How do you believe people change? How have you changed? Here you reflect on your own Christian experience. What have you seen happen in others such as the role of prayer, Bible teaching, one to one conversations, God's work and ours?

Suffering

Often the most poignant moments in life come through tough times: illness, bereavement, foolishness leading to unwanted consequences, aspirations not fulfilled, job loss, broken relationships and so on.

Add your thoughts to the following grid:

BACKGROUND	
EXPERIENCE (including life events)	
RELATIONSHIP WITH GOD	
GIFTINGS	
VALUES	
BELIEFS ABOUT PEOPLE AND HOW THEY CHANGE	
SUFFERING	

The iceberg model

Most of what we bring to the coaching and mentoring relationship is 'below the waterline', ie not readily observable. This is also true of the coachee and mentoree.

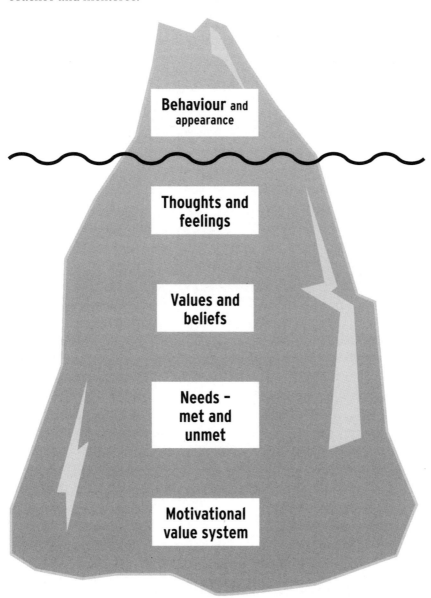

Why might it be appropriate to 'lower the waterline' with your coachee? Just as you have reflected upon what you bring to the coaching and mentoring relationship, your coachee and mentoree will bring their own approach to life too. You will need to be aware of this as you coach and mentor if you are to make true progress.

---

[1] Oxford Brookes University Coaching and Mentoring Society (OBCAMS).
[2] Tony Stoltzfus, *Leadership Coaching* (Booksurge Publishing, 2005).

PART ONE:

Coaching

OI:

Introduction to coaching

We focus exclusively on coaching in this chapter and the next. It's useful to know the way the word 'coaching' developed. In the 1500s the word 'coach' described a horse-drawn vehicle that would get people from where they were to where they wanted to be. Today the horse power is found in the engine of a vehicle with the same goal. In the 1880s, the word 'coach' was given an athletic meaning when it was used to identify the person who tutored university students in their rowing on the Cam River in Cambridge. The word stuck and coaches became known as people who help athletes move from one place to another. Over time the word also became associated with the person who helped musicians, public speakers and actors to improve their skills, overcome obstacles, remain focused, and get to where they want to be. In the 1990s in particular, coaching spread from sports and entertainment to the world of business.

In companies large and small, people at all levels had to learn how to deal with change, develop new management styles, make wise decisions and become more effective, all while they coped with their hyperactive lifestyles and increasing stress. HR leaders have found that coaching can provide help to employees faster and more efficiently than if they sent them on training courses.

As Malcolm Knowles said: 'One of the most significant things about adult learning research is that when adults learn something naturally instead of "being taught" they are highly self-directing (they feel ownership and act on it). What adults learn on their own initiative they learn more keenly and permanently than what they learn by being taught.'[1]

Today people are turning to nutritional coaches, fitness coaches, financial coaches, public-speaking coaches, and what have become known as life coaches, who help others find focus and direction for their lives and careers.

We have already noted that there is no universal definition for the word coaching.

It is used to describe the process whereby an expert imparts their skills to someone aiming to improve. This is typically through the expert demonstrating the activity (as in golf or tennis) so that the coachee can imitate, and receive feedback. In this book we are using the word mentoring to describe this directed activity.

We use the coaching definition more commonly used within the fields of executive coaching and life coaching. A coach seeks to facilitate the growth and progress in someone through non-directive conversation.

The heart of a coach

Anyone can bake a cake. You buy the ingredients, follow the recipe and the oven does the rest. Many assume that anyone can coach because the skills required are similarly within the reach of most of us. That's partly true; most people can 'listen and ask questions', but there is an element to coaching that is intrinsic to who you are.

Coaching is more than mixing together a few skills and hey presto, someone is helped. Coaching has many skills that we can learn, but at the very heart of coaching is that intangible but real quality that must shine through: a concern for a person's growth and development.

Coaches care about other people. A Christian is already growing in this quality. We are all a 'work in progress' and we can all say that we are growing in our appreciation of all that God has done for us in Christ. We know forgiveness for sins and are discovering the riches of walking with God, indwelt by His Spirit. We are turning from a self-focused agenda to serve God's agenda of restoring all things to Himself. We are learning to work in the world for His kingdom, and this includes, of course, an agenda that involves caring for others' wellbeing; being freed from competition with others, jealousy of others gifts, and fear that we might be left behind. We can be glad when others succeed and flourish, and discover who they are and what they can be. The old cliché is true: 'they don't care how much you know, they want to know how much you care!'

If this all sounds as though a coach needs to be a mix between the angel Gabriel and Mother Teresa, don't be despondent. We will grow in the degree of care as we get to know the coachee and learn to trust God as we coach.

What we have said is not for one moment suggesting that those who do not have a Christian faith are not 'others focused' too. Many of other faiths and none outshine many Christians in the depth of their care for those they help. But we are saying that if you do know Christ, you have His help and example to draw on, which can assist you as you give yourself to others.

Take a look at the following statements, labelled 'A' and 'B'.

'A' statements
- I am often comparing myself with others
- I easily become jealous when I see other people succeed
- I wonder why I do not seem to flourish in my life
- I think that people ought to sort things out on their own if they are talented

'B' statements
- I like to play a part in people resolving issues
- I think everyone has potential that needs unlocking
- I am sad to think of people stuck in situations that they don't need to be in
- I enjoy listening to people's hopes and dreams and love to see them realised

If you resonate more with statements A than B you may want to consider this before you engage in coaching. It can take a long time to grasp who we are in Christ and feel secure enough to be others focused. Our default mode is to be self focused. We fear that we might lose out if we don't look after ourselves. God really has looked after everything through the life and death and resurrection of Jesus. It is as if we have £1,000,000 in our spiritual account. We don't have to 'work' anymore and are free to give our time and energy to others, so they can realise how rich they are too. Why not ask God to change your heart to be more others focused?

What a coach provides

You can assess your potential 'coaching capacity' by looking at the following things that a good coach looks to provide:

Perspective

Someone knows they are not making progress in an area and wants to discover what's holding them back in order to deal with it. You give them space to stand back and observe what is going in their life.

Structure

You provide a structured session for working through a situation. They know that the problem that has been bothering them will be addressed in the regular coaching session and this frees them to focus on other things.

Accountability

You hold the coachee accountable to do what they have promised. Your detachment enables you to encourage the coachee into action in a way that most friends and family members would find awkward.

Encouragement

In the course of the conversation, you and the coachee identify where progress can be made and provide a basis on which you give personal encouragement, as the coachee takes steps towards a solution.

Listening

In some cases the coachee has no one who will actively listen to them in an accepting environment committed to progress. Your listening is a vital part of the process, irrespective of what you say!

Hope

Often a coachee will have faced unease over their situation for some time and fear that little can be done to change things. You can say: 'it doesn't have to be this way.'

Reflecting on what we have considered, can you say, at least in measure, that your heart is towards others; that you see people as image bearers with potential and a capacity to grow to be more than who they are at present?

What kind of things do coaches help with?

You may have gathered that coaching can be utilised to help the coachee make progress in a whole range of areas: it might be improving their performance at work, developing better friendships, managing a career change, helping their relationship with a child, losing weight or a host of other areas.

Christians have been coached through the discovery and utilisation of gifts, dealing with an awkward co-worker, handling stress, managing time, sharing their faith, improving public speaking, managing personal finances, rebooting struggling personal devotions, to mention just a few of the many areas.

How do coaches work?

Through conversation the coach will identify the outcomes that the coachee is seeking and help set goals for them to work towards. The coach provides support and accountability as the coachee decides on the goals, and works towards completing them. Such conversations are orchestrated by the coach as they guide the coachee into finding solutions themselves. We look at how good listening and questioning accomplish this in the next two chapters.

As we have noted already, we are using a non-directive approach. This may seem slow at first, especially if you have been used to offering advice. Occasionally those who attend coaching courses at CWR have expressed irritation at this approach: 'why don't you just tell them what to do?' The approach may seem slow, but it can be very satisfying. Yes, you could make someone's decision for them, or you can help them make better decisions for the rest of their life!

The length of conversation and frequency of meeting will vary according to the situation being discussed and the progress being made. A series of 45-minute conversations every week for a six-week period might be useful for one person; an hour fortnightly for three months might be suitable for another. Some coaches work face to face, others over the phone or via Skype. Fees vary, with some coaches being able to offer their services free, some offering a reduced cost to Christians, others charging the going rate. It is really important to have clarity on the 'contract' between coach and coachee at the beginning or you may find that you both have very different expectations.

The eventual goal is to help the coachee to take action – as the saying goes, 'if the coacheee isn't taking action, you aren't coaching!'

If I had to identify four key words for coaching they would be 'asking, listening, acting and supporting'. We will look later at the skills the coach learns to help the coachee find solutions and approaches to what they are facing, and at the ways of structuring conversations to get the desired outcomes.

Jesus – a coach?

Although the word coaching is never used in Jesus' ministry, there were elements of non-directive coaching in the way He worked with His Twelve disciples. He would often ask questions and encourage them to take action rather than tell them exactly what to do. He asked them to reflect on life experience, rather as a coach would. Jesus knew the value of allowing His followers to figure things out at their own pace and in their own time. Sadly, we don't have a record of many detailed conversations between Jesus and any of the Twelve. This was not the purpose of the Gospel writers. But we have enough hints in His interaction to know that He would have used coaching-type approaches on occasions.

For example, Jesus asks the disciples to feed the crowds: 'You give them something to eat' (Matt 14:16).

He knew that He intended to feed them by multiplying the bread and fish, but to start with He placed the dilemma at their feet, knowing that it would create a tension within them that would help them appreciate the final answer better.

He asks the Twelve: 'Who do people say the Son of Man is?' (Matt. 16:13).

He wanted them to reflect on the messages they were hearing on the ground, and what they themselves thought.

In his reinstatement of Simon Peter, Jesus initially asks him to review their relationship: 'Simon son of John, do you love me more than these?' (John 21:14). He could have simply assured Simon Peter that he had forgiven Peter for denying Him, but He chooses instead to ask questions that would help Peter reflect on his situation.

Most of the time Jesus is far more directive than a coach would be. He is, after all, leading the Twelve and all who would follow Him into a new kind of behaviour. So it is more of a mentoring than a coaching relationship. But as we will see, good mentoring will include coaching approaches too.

The coaching relationship

The diagram below outlines two key elements to developing a good coaching relationship: clarity and rapport. Both are vital to the process. Rapport is built by a willingness to participate in the relationship and commitment to it, and usually leads to the relationship being enjoyable as well as effective. Having a broad sense of purpose builds clarity as to the anticipated results of meeting together.

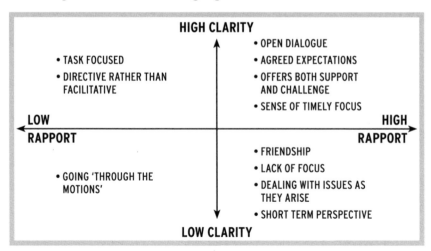

Adapted from 'The relationship between goal clarity and rapport in mentoring' in *Mentoring and Diversity* by Clutterbuck and Ragins (Routledge, 2001).

[1] Malcolm Knowles, *Designs for Adult Learning* (American Society for Training & Development, 1995).

02:

Vital coaching skills: Listening

At the heart of coaching and mentoring are skills that most of us began to learn on the first day of school. Can you remember back to that first day, when you were told to listen carefully and if you have a question, put your hand up? In this chapter we are going to check whether your listening skills have progressed from that first day's schooling and in the following chapter show you the kind of questions that will unlock an exciting future for yourself and those you coach.

Listening

Listening does not come easily for most of us. We fail to listen properly to people for a variety of reasons:

- We think we know what the person is saying, maybe because we have heard something like it before.
- We make a quick judgment in our minds: studies show that the average doctor diagnoses the problem within just 13 seconds of hearing the problem expressed by the patient. Most of us do much the same.
- We are involved in other things as we try to listen, and so don't give the person speaking our full attention.

- We partly hear what is being said, but spend most of the listening time thinking about what to say in response. Have you ever overheard a conversation on public transport where it was clear that neither person was actually listening to the other?

All these mean we fail to truly hear and understand what we are told.

How can you listen as a coach?

TURNING OFF THE JUDGMENT SWITCH

Most of us fail to listen in a way that can enhance the coaching process. We make mental judgments as we listen that interfere with our capacity to listen in a way that moves the coaching process forward. Remember, coaching is a non-directive process which works on the assumption that the coachee has the answers and our job is to help them take the appropriate next action to address their issues.

Imagine that our coachee is telling us a story of an interaction with a friend and his angry response. We might be thinking 'Oh, I would never have done that', or 'yep, fair enough, that makes sense.'

Making that sort of snap judgment is unavoidable. It's part of who you are.

But you need to turn off the judgment taking place in your head so it doesn't interfere with your capacity to hear, and most importantly, to serve the person you are listening to. Your job is to understand what you are hearing, in the context of the issue that your coachee wants to discuss, and help them grasp more fully what is going on and what may be holding them back – ie to understand the problem and think about solutions.

When you find yourself jumping to make judgments or draw conclusions, you are better using that moment as a time to be curious. This is especially true if you feel in any way awkward, uncomfortable or disapproving of what you hear. Use that moment as a potential conversation point if, and only if, it serves you to better understand the person in the context of the topic.

Let us illustrate this by recounting a person's story who wanted to be coached about his job.

I am not sure what to make of my job. On the one hand working in sales gives me great benefits and a comfortable lifestyle. I am not stressed and can do my job smoothly. On the other hand I come home some days and my conscience bothers me. I get my calls done so early I can get home two hours before the end of my working day: a quarter of the day doing nothing and yet paid for the whole day!

I have asked my boss about it, but he says not to worry – that's just the way the job is. But it doesn't seem very moral and I feel as if I am letting God down.

As you read that scenario, you will have instantly made a judgment. Maybe you wonder what on earth he is worried about. Maybe you are thinking, 'lucky guy, I wish I had a job like that!' Or perhaps you sympathise with the dilemma?

Here's some questions that could be asked, but wouldn't help.

Q. How could you let go of responsibility for things that are beyond your control?
This is a question based on a judgment you have made and a solution you are offering.

Q. It seems God has given you a mini holiday every day. Couldn't you just accept it?
Again, this is a question that flows from a judgment that you have made. Worse still you are questioning whether he should feel bad.

Q. How could you help your boss see that his thinking is wrong?
This question attempts to sympathise with the coachee but ends up making a judgment on what the solution should be. This is not the coach's job.

Q. Given the chance, what would you change about the system?
This question is better. It explores the issue with the coachee. It helps give them a handle on whether there are things that could be changed and maybe edges towards them knowing what it is they need to do. Some coaches call this process of listening, 'listening with intuition'. You are seeking to spot what the person is actually saying.

Listening 'intuitively'

You listen intuitively when you look for what the coachee is telling you in what they say. Specifically, this includes the following:

- The person's own discernment
- Turning points or key actions
- Strong emotions or reaction
- Red lights – things that don't seem to fit
- Patterns – cause and effect.

Of these, the person's own discernment is the most important element. Registering the coachee's own assessment of what is going on is key. Even if they do not have an accurate assessment, this will be the place to start.

See if you can spot the things to note in this story.

Case Study

University was my chance to get away from home and make my own decisions in life. But it was hard being in such a big place, having grown up in a small Dorset village. Back home everyone knew each other, here there were thousands of students. At home I was the fastest runner in the school and a lead actor in school plays, but at university I was a nobody. No one noticed how I did on my course work – so why not just loaf around instead of working? I think that is what messed me up – I felt alone and irrelevant.

In the autumn, I met Jan. She was the first person I really confided in. She liked me as I was and stuck by me. By the spring term we started to go out on dates and it was clear that I was in love with her. The first time she talked about marriage I became very scared. Mum and Dad had been at one another's throats and I didn't know if I wanted that sort of commitment. And Jan's faith bothered me. She was very much into Christianity and I was more cynical, wanting to be a little less OTT. She kept urging me to be more serious about God. I knew she was right but I kept putting it off. I guess I wanted God on my terms, not on His.

Over the summer she went on a short-term mission trip and wrote to say that she'd had an experience with God. When I got back to university in the autumn term I was keen to start off where we had left off but she told me she didn't want to be with someone as lukewarm as me.

I was devastated. I spent the next few days in a fog – I turned up for a lecture one day and no one was there – I had the wrong day! That night I went for a walk by myself and said: 'God, my life isn't working. I can't keep playing this game with You – I'm miserable. If You are real, make Yourself real to me, because I don't know who You are.'

Nothing magical happened at that moment, but I started reading my Bible and praying seriously again. And then these amazing coincidences started to take place …

Questions

What would you want to explore? Which key phrases would you pick up on?

Answers

As you go through, you can identify areas to pick up on if you are listening properly.

Here is the same story again, but with notes on parts which stand out:

University was my chance to get away from home *(DISCERNMENT: he uses the word 'chance' – why?)* and make my own decisions in life *(TURNING POINT: leaving home is always a key turning point, but may be worth exploring)*. But it was hard being in such a big place, having grown up in a small Dorset village. Back home everyone knew each other, here there were thousands of students. At home I was the fastest runner in the school and a lead actor in school plays, but at university I was a nobody *(DISCERNMENT: He uses a strong word to describe how he feels)*.

No one noticed how I did on my course work – so why not just loaf around instead of working? I think that is what messed me up – I felt alone and irrelevant *(DISCERNMENT: his understanding of what was going on)*.

In the autumn, I met Jan *(TURNING POINT: this is the subject of the conversation, so needs exploring)*.

She was the first person I really confided in. She liked me as I was and stuck by me. By the spring term we started to go out on dates and it was clear that I was in love with her *(EMOTIONS: you might ask how he knew? Had he been in love before?)*.

The first time she talked about marriage I became very scared *(RED LIGHT: this seems unusual – a little premature to talk about marriage after such a relatively short time)*.

Mum and Dad had been at one another's throats and I didn't know if I wanted that sort of commitment *(CAUSE AND EFFECT: he assumes that his feelings about marriage are connected to his parents' struggles)*.

And Jan's faith bothered me. She was very much into Christianity and I was more cynical, wanting to be a little less OTT. She kept urging me to be more serious about God. I knew she was right but I kept putting it off. I guess I wanted God on my terms, not on His *(DISCERNMENT: his view of his spiritual life)*.

Over the summer she went on a short-term mission trip and wrote to say that she'd had an experience with God. When I got back to university in the autumn term I was keen to start off where we had left off but she told me she didn't want to be with someone as lukewarm as me *(TURNING POINT: clearly a tough time)*.

I was devastated *(EMOTIONS: strong language to describe how he felt)*. I spent the next few days in a fog – I turned up for a lecture one day and no one was there – I had the wrong day!

That night I went for a walk by myself and said: 'God, my life isn't working. I can't keep playing this game with You – I'm miserable. If You are real, make Yourself real to me, because I don't know who You are.' *(RED LIGHT: it seems odd that he should turn to God in prayer, having been apparently 'cynical' before.)*

Nothing magical happened at that moment, but I started reading my Bible and praying seriously again. And then these amazing coincidences started to take place … *(TURNING POINT: it would be worth exploring what these were)*.

In practice, the goal of the conversation will determine how much weight would be given to each point above, but a good listener would be able to pick up on those elements.

If you know that you are not an especially good listener, don't despair. You can become better and will improve when you realise that your good listening and discerning questioning based on your listening are giving insights. I have a friend who works as an 'Executive Coach' and talks about the satisfying 'aha' moments that make his job worthwhile. You can literally turn someone's life around if you listen well. It's worth persevering.

Most of us can practise our listening skills quite comfortably in our daily life. You would be surprised what a difference it can make to a marriage, relationships with children, friendships, work with colleagues. Why not make it an aim to practise your listening skills in the next 24 hours and see how you do?

O3:

Vital coaching skills: Questioning

We turn in this chapter to look at the kinds of questions we ask to help the coachee explore the issue or topic at hand. Questions are valuable for us as we seek to better understand the person and the situation or issue that they are concerned with. They are also vital for the coachee as we aim to give them self-understanding and opportunity to probe more deeply.

Types of questions

There are two broad categories of questions: closed-ended and open-ended questions.

A 'closed' question is one that requires a single word or short phrase response. Journalists learn to avoid these questions, especially when they suspect the interviewee (maybe a sports person or celebrity) is awkward. A closed-ended question will not take things forward. For example:

- Are you feeling better than last time? The coachee can say 'yes' or 'no'.
- Did you do what we said you would do last week? The coachee can say 'yes' or 'no'.

An open-ended question would take things forward. For example:

- How are you feeling today compared to the last time we met?
- Last time we agreed some action points; how did you find them?

Both these questions require the coachees to think. The answer provides you useful information to better understand the situation and how you might progress.

Solution-oriented questions

Your aim is to help the coachee to come up with the solutions themselves, so solution-oriented questions, which imply the answer, are generally not appropriate. They dis-empower the coachee and effectively ask for agreement to a proposition, rather than respecting their capacity to think and decide for themselves.

For example, consider these two solution-oriented questions:

- Could you find information on that through the internet?
- Would it work to take a day off and finish that project?

The question includes the solution you think they should take. Your job is not to provide solutions but to lead them. Your solutions may be no help to them anyway.

It would be better to say, 'Where might you find that information?' or 'What are the ways you could consider that would speed the project on?'

There may be occasions when a solution or an aspect of the situation presents itself to you, which is not apparent to the coachee. You ask appropriate questions, but the coachee may have internally discounted various options before even exploring them. On such occasions, my colleague Bev has used a statement along the lines of: 'Can I take my coach's hat off for a moment? Is there a reason why x is not an option you are considering?'

As a one-off or occasional intervention, this is perfectly acceptable, though it is the kind of thing more common in mentoring than coaching. You would need to make it clear that any solutions you offer in such circumstances need to be owned by the coachee, and not adopted because you have offered them. That said, you wouldn't be offering it if you didn't think it had merit.

Kinds of questions

Coaching has some wonderful types of open-ended questions that can be part of your questioning arsenal.

- Probing questions: explore the drama.
- Awareness questions: help the coachee identify what is happening.
- Revealing questions: change perspective away from limitations.
- Bigger questions: expand the focus.
- The miracle question: identifies solutions.
- Motivating questions: aim to spur the coachee on.
- Direct questions: cut to the heart of an issue.
- Ownership questions: pushes the coachee to own their part and be proactive.

We will explore these below.

Don't be alarmed by the variety of types of question. You don't need to learn them all. Over time, a coach will know intuitively the sort of questions to ask that will help the coachee explore the topic and decide on the action he or she intends to take. These questions give you an idea of the kind of approaches you can take.

PROBING QUESTIONS

The word 'probing' may create an image of a hostile questioner. You may have in mind the kind of questioning perfected by BBC presenter, Jeremy Paxman. He has a reputation for persisting with a line of enquiry, created in part by his repeated questioning of Conservative MP, Michael Howard, in 1997 after he was accused of illegally threatening the head of Britain's Prison Service, Derek Lewis. He asked the same question twelve times!

Coaches are not probing in that sense – remember it is not your job to extract something that you believe the coachee may be trying to hide – but the coachee has given tacit permission to probe, by virtue of entering the coaching relationship.

Probing questions in coaching:

- use the client's own words
- are succinct
- are neutral

These questions are the 'bread and butter' questions of coaching. You will probably use a probing question every time you coach.

Examples of probing questions

- Tell me a little more about that
- Give me some background – what led up to this situation?
- When you think about … what kind of feelings does it bring up?
- You mentioned … tell me more about …
- What did you mean when you said ...?
- What was most significant to you in this experience?
- What would be most important for us to focus on?
- How did that happen?

Imagine a coachee comes to you and says the following:

> I feel like life is going well. The new job is fine and my boss is happy. Not only am I meeting expectations, I am exceeding them. A few days ago my boss even told me I was doing good work. I really love being valued for who I am and how much I do, instead of just putting my head down and being ignored.
>
> The major hassle is the commute. It is 40 minutes more than I had before and the workday is much longer, so I am out over an hour more. So I get little time to myself and feel robbed. I get home and there's a million things to do, plus the children to play with. Then June wants attention. By the time it gets to 10pm I am just about ready to crash.

Using probing questions you might ask:

- Tell me more about what you love about being valued?

- You say you felt robbed. What would be a healthy amount of personal time for you?
- Sounds like your new job is going well apart from how it affects your time. Can you say a bit more about it?

What is wrong with the following questions?

1. Why did you take that job in the first place?
2. Tell me about how you've allowed your job to rob you of your personal time?
3. You mentioned that you loved being valued. How has this need affected your family life?

Answers

These questions do not probe according to what the coachee has shared but are based on presumptions made by you, the coach. It may be interesting to know why the job was taken, but such a question implies that the coachee should have foreseen the commuting problems. A better question would be: what were the pros and cons you could see when you took the job? They may have been unemployed for a year and so delighted to have a job offer that they hoped the commute wouldn't be a problem.

Characteristics of probing questions

The coachee must not feel threatened, misunderstood or forced into a corner.

Your aim is to extend the coachee's thinking process, not insert your thoughts. Probing questions enable the coachee to explore the situation further and deeper.

Note that questions which start 'Why' can be hard to use without implying a judgment, so many coaches avoid using them altogether.

Such probing questions can be used outside of the coaching situation, of course. You can use them to help family and friends, too.

SELF-AWARENESS QUESTIONS

Coaching helps people take responsibility for their life within the framework of trust and dependence on God. But the crucial prerequisite for taking responsibility is their own awareness of what is happening in the first place, and studies prove that most people are very poor at self-evaluation.

In *Coaching for Performance*[1], John Whitmore looks at asking effective questions so that the coachee is able to become more aware of what is going on. He uses illustrations from the world of tennis which translate into all areas of coaching. He suggests that some questions are very ineffective and looks at the oft-quoted maxim in sports that it is important to watch the ball. He imagines the coach's question:

'Are you watching the ball?'

How would we respond to that? He suggests, defensively, perhaps, and we might be tempted to lie as we did at school when the teacher asked us if we were paying attention!

'Why are you not watching the ball?'

More defensiveness – or perhaps a little analysis if you are that inclined. 'I am', 'I don't know', 'because I was thinking about my grip' or, more truthfully, 'because you are distracting me and making me nervous'.

These are not very effective questions, but consider the effect of the following:

- Which way is the ball spinning as it comes towards you?
- How high is it this time as it crosses the net?
- Does it spin faster or slower after it bounces, this time – each time?
- How far is it from your opponent when you first see which way it is spinning?

These questions are of a different order. They create four important effects that neither the other questions nor commands do:

These types of questions **compel the player** to watch the ball. It is not possible to answer the question unless he or she does that.

The player will have to **focus to a higher order** than normal to give the accurate answer the question demands, providing a higher quality of input.

The answers sought are **descriptive, not judgmental**, so there is no risk of descent into self-criticism or damage to self-esteem.

We have the benefit of a **feedback loop for the coach**, who is able to verify the accuracy of the player's answer, and therefore the quality of concentration.

Coaching can help the coachee to become aware of what they are doing, by careful questioning.

A parallel illustration when coaching a Christian would be: instead of asking, 'do you pray?', which might create a defensive response, ask, 'are there times in the week when you think about talking to God?' or 'when might you be tempted to talk to God?'

Instead of asking, 'why don't you share your faith more?' ask, 'when would you be most likely to want to talk about your faith?'

In both cases the coachee is describing their life, not made to feel that something should or shouldn't happen. It helps them reflect on themselves and in reflecting, find information, which might lead to a solution.

Asking permission

If you feel it is appropriate to enter a new area or look at a sensitive issue, it's important to ask permission. This question could be used at any stage, of course, but especially in the early stages, when you are building mutual trust.

- Would it be OK if we probed that area?
- That statement caught my attention. I realise it may be sensitive, but could you explore that?
- That sounded pretty strong. You seem to feel this deeply?

REVEALING QUESTIONS

People come to coaching because they feel stuck and are asking you to unstick them. They are often unable to find a solution because they have made unwarranted assumptions about themselves and the world around them. Coaching manuals have various terms for this: some see it as like living in a box. Others talk of 'interferences': something is interfering with the progress that they can make. This might be circumstances, beliefs, or rules. So experienced coaches are curious about the coachee's patterns of behaviour which indicate the limitations they are working under.

Common boxes:

- time
- confidence
- networks
- responsibilities
- money

Once you have identified a box, name it and ask the coachee to think outside it, or re-examine whether it can be changed.

For example, a coachee might say to you: 'I can't get to the mission field until I pay off six years worth of debt'. They are making assumptions based on the time they believe it will take. They may be correct, but it's worth asking: 'How could you cut this time in half?'

Or they may be saying that they can't find the time to study. So you could ask: 'If you had to give up something that would free up three hours a week, what would it be?'

There are many 'confidence' boxes.

You are chatting with a coachee and they say, 'I could never stand up in front of people and speak!' Gentle questioning might include: 'Have you ever had to? What happened? Could you *read* in front of people?'

Sometimes the coachee feels too alone to make the kind of decisions they need to take, or get the resources they need. They say, 'But I don't know anyone who can help me!'

You could ask: 'Do you know anyone who is well connected? Could they introduce you?'

Don't be afraid of silences. They may indicate that you are helping the coachee to think.

On each occasion you are gently questioning the assumptions they are making. They may be correct for them at that moment, but they may be limiting their actions. In my first ever session as a coachee, I began to understand that I was limited by what I came to realise was a restrictive view of God's will. I was scared of taking action in case I got it wrong, when the issue in question might easily have been a good one to take.

A coaching situation

Here's a coachee's testimony:

> Last Autumn I was feeling overwhelmed with everything I needed to do. None of the tasks could wait and I saw no prospect of any relief. It would be a grind until Christmas and I would have to just pray that God would not send anything else for me to do. I met with a coach but I wasn't expecting any help because these things were fixed – work, home, ministry responsibilities in church. But the coach asked me a question that I decided to adopt

as an action step: 'what would reduce your stress by 50 per cent?'
I prayed about this and set aside some time to think. The question
started to free me up. I realised that the strain came not from
the activities but from a fear of failure. I didn't like being a
disappointment, at home, at work and especially at church,
because the people there have been so good to me. I also didn't
want to disappoint myself and especially God. I realised that I
could reduce my stress by not taking responsibility for things that
God had not called me to take responsibility for.

So I gave up being fearful and defensive and believing that life
would only be good and restful if such-and-such happened. I
decided that I could know joy and rest in the present, rather than
adopting a discouraged outlook.

You don't need to come up with a strategy to remove the block, but use
it as an exercise to imagine the future. Then ask the coachee to see how
much of that ideal life they could keep.

Revealing questions – examples

These are called revealing questions because they reveal what you could
do or be if a limitation was removed.

A classic revealing question would be: imagine that what is in the way
is removed; what would the future look like without it?

You might also want to try the following:

- If you knew you couldn't fail, what would you do?
- If you knew you had unlimited resources, how would that
  change your approach?
- If your hurt went away, how would you respond?
- If you had four more hours in a day, what would you do?

ASKING BIGGER QUESTIONS

Part of helping people think 'outside the box' is to ask big questions – ie
open up the question away from the narrow frame of reference.

Someone comes to you to ask whether they should take a promotion.
You could ask: 'OK – you are not sure whether to take the promotion.
What sort of job would you like?'

You might catch yourself being diagnostic. Don't ask a weighted question so that the coachee is forced to come to your way of thinking – ask a bigger question.

For example: you think they need an accountant. Instead of saying 'have you thought of getting an accountant?' ask, 'can you think of anyone who could help you?'

THE MIRACLE QUESTION

If the coachee is struggling to articulate what they would like to see happen in them, you might try using the miracle question technique.

You say to the coachee:

> Suppose that whilst you are asleep tonight a miracle occurs, and you have all the changes you wanted to get from coaching. Because you are asleep, you don't know that the miracle has happened. What would be the first sign for you after you wake up which will tell you that the miracle has happened?

The key to using this successfully is to help the person you are working with to be extremely precise about the specific changes they will notice in their feelings, thoughts, internal images, sensations, and so on. Do this by asking them questions about the details of their experience. To answer these questions they will have to create for themselves the experience of already having made the changes they are seeking – and so the 'miracle' occurs!

MOTIVATING QUESTIONS

These questions help people identify and pursue what they believe they are called to. They won't always be appropriate, but they do open up the discussion if you sense that the coachee could usefully explore where life is heading. Motivating questions can be very powerful. I had a boss who once asked me, 'Andy, if money was no object, what would you do with your life?' It's a powerful big question. Why not consider it as you read this? Get's you thinking, doesn't it?

Here are some more motivating questions:

• What do you most want to be or accomplish before you die?
• Think of a situation where you could imagine yourself saying,

'this is what I was born for'. Describe it to me.
- Who are the people you are most drawn to help?
- What is stopping you from pursuing your dreams now? What could you do about that?
- What are you passionate about – what sort of job would make you want to leap out of bed in the morning?
- Where do you want to be in a year? Five years?
- What have you done in life which you thought was worthwhile?

DIRECT QUESTIONS

There are times when it is right to use a more direct question. They will typically come at the end of the conversation when you are confident that you have the measure of the coachee and can safely move the conversation on with a more direct approach. It is critical that we get this right. If your emotions get in the way and you start getting involved in making judgments, the coachee will start reacting to you and the message will be lost.

Case study

'So, how's things today, Joe?'

'OK, ta.'

'You said you wanted to see me about coaching? I trust you received the stuff I emailed you.'

'Yes.'

'Any problems?'

'No, that's fine. It clarified what coaching is. I am cool with it.'

'Good. What do you want to talk about?'

'Well, I have been watching a Christian TV channel and one of the preachers there was talking about exercising faith and seeing great things happen, in life, relationships and finances. So I was figuring time with you might enable me to go up a gear.'

'How do you mean?'

'Well, have a greater income.'

'OK. What specifically did the preacher say?'

'He was talking about ten-fold increases. I earn 16k, so I figure 160k is where I am heading!'

Ineffective direct questions

- These TV preachers don't know what they are talking about. How could you have fallen for that?
- Do you find Jesus urging His followers to having a ten-fold increase in earnings?

Effective direct questions

- Have you ever heard a preacher who would say the opposite to this preacher?
- How did the preacher justify his explanation to you?
- This message seems very similar to self-help books written by people who are not Christians. Is there any difference here?
- Would you expect there to be a difference?

When I was leading a course and used this example I had assumed that those present on the course would regard the young man's desire for a 160k salary as foolish. I was surprised to discover that more than a few thought this was OK!

Nevertheless, I stand by the questions asked above. In some cases, these kinds of aspirations are appealing to our baser instincts, even as I acknowledge that increased wealth is not evil and can and should be used for kingdom benefit.

You can be direct providing you honour the coachee and allow them to make the decisions.

Good direct questions challenge without using guilt, shame or intimidation. They avoid the word 'why' and point towards a positive outcome. Good direct questions are about the coachee's growth, not the coach's agenda. They don't accuse, they inquire.

Direct questions exercise

Turn these lousy questions into questions that can take the conversation forward:

- When are you going to cotton on that you can't overstretch yourself?
- Why can't you just do the actions we talked about, like everyone else?

- Didn't we discuss that last week?
- Why did you get mad and lose it over that?
- Why on earth would you even contemplate taking that sort of job?
- Should you be spending Sundays at cricket or church?
- Do you really think that more money is going to make your marriage work?

OWNERSHIP QUESTIONS

God wants us to own up to the part of situations and problems which we need to own. Often we are reluctant to own up to our part. The problem is 'out there' or 'with them'. Ownership questions help people own up to their part. They are used in conflict situations and also when constructing action steps.

Examples of ownership questions:

- What do you want to do about this?
- What step do you want to take?
- How do you want to go about that?
- What do you think the answer is?

You encourage the coachee to be responsible, proactive, and work things out with God.

PUTTING INTO PRACTICE

Dana works as a doctor in a medical practice in town. She visited a Christian conference and came back convinced that God wanted her to become a missionary. When you ask her to outline why she wants to be coached, she says:

> I believe I am meant to go overseas, but at the moment I am very afraid of the next step. I love it here and the thought of overseas travel terrifies me. I have only ever been to France, and that was as a child with my parents. But I guess I am even more afraid that my walk with God will suffer if I don't follow it up.

What sort of questions might you ask?

Later in the conversation she says:

> I'm in love with a guy in the church. I am not sure if he likes me,
> or is even aware of me. I know I need to resolve this if I am to
> make progress with becoming a missionary. Also, I am keen to see
> my niece grow up – she's 14 months old – and I hate the thought
> of disappearing for years on end, and missing her development.
> It's only when you have the prospect of losing something that you
> realise what matters. Money is no problem for me – I have some
> savings, but my church is quite small and already supports one
> missionary. I am not sure how they would respond to another one.
> But then I am not too sure that I want them to say yes anyway!

What blocks are evident?

In the chapter on listening we saw that blocks include the following:

- The person's own discernment
- Turning points or key actions
- Strong emotions or reaction
- Red lights – things that don't seem to fit
- Patterns – cause and effect.

What questions could help her around the blocks?

Further questioning reveals that the 'call' came when a preacher at
one of the events challenged people with skills needed in the Third World
to offer them to God.

> At the end of the talk he said that anyone who had skills which
> they hadn't surrendered to God should stand up as an indication
> that they meant business.
> I have never done this before, and so stood up to offer my medical
> training to God to do whatever He wanted. I was shaking like a
> leaf, because I wasn't too sure what might happen.

As Dana finishes the time with you it is clear that the process of talking
the situation through has upset her. She is feeling very torn with the
emotional and psychological pressures she is facing.

'I have only been in the practice eight months. Does God really want to me to jack it all in? I am not sure I could cope.'

What sort of things would you say which would encourage her to take some action steps?

Answers

Probing questions would be helpful for Dana to begin with, for example:

- How did the 'call' come about?
- Have you ever had a call like this before?
- When you say 'overseas' do you have anywhere in mind at this stage?
- You say that your 'walk with God would suffer'. How would that be?

What blocks are evident?

Dana is not sure about the guy she likes at church, frightened about missing out on her niece's growth and how the church would respond to her going on an international missionary trip.

What revealing questions could help her around the blocks?

You could ask what would assure her of the guy's feelings for her. Has she had a relationship before? What kind of question could she ask him that might progress things, without making things awkward?

She mentions 'disappearing for years on end'. This suggests an old-fashioned understanding of missions work where you may be gone 'years'. You might want to ask her of what she thinks mission work might entail.

You could ask her if she knows anyone on the Missions Committee with whom she might be able to talk things through.

It may seem intimidating to look at the myriad of kinds of questions above. You won't be able to stop the questioner mid flow and search for this book. Over time you will instinctively know the kind of questions to ask. In the moment of the conversation you will take your cue from what they say of course, so it will seem like a natural conversation. Good reflection on how it went can help you improve, and that will come with time and experience.

[1] John Whitmore, *Coaching for Performance* (Third Edition), (London: Nicholas Brealey Publishing, 2002).

04:

Tools for structuring the conversation

Having noted some of the conversation skills we need to develop, we turn now to consider how the conversation itself may develop. We have all had conversations that didn't turn out the way we expected. How can we ensure that this time is of mutual benefit?

Many coaches follow a structure for the conversation. A structure can be especially useful in your early days as a coach, but even experienced coaches still use one or a number of structures to facilitate their chat.

The GROW (or TGROW) model is one of the most popular. It was devised by Sir John Whitmore in the classic book *Coaching for Performance*, which first appeared in 1990.

The GROW model

'GROW' is a mnemonic that defines a framework for analysis. Often the letter T is added at the start.

The acronym expands like this:

T is for Topic

This denotes the area the coachee wants to explore via coaching. Example topics might be social life, career, or dealing with a pattern of behaviour.

The coach and coachee may agree on a topic before starting, but deciding on what the particular topic might be would be the subject matter of the first session.

G is for Goal

The client is encouraged to turn a problem statement into a positive desired outcome, then to embody this into a goal. The goal should be made as real and specific as possible and, ideally, will be SMART (Specific, Measurable, Attainable, Relevant and Time-specific).

R is for Reality

The client is encouraged to explore the problem (defined by the Topic and the Goal) and other aspects of their life to gain a fact-based and current understanding of how things really are.

O is for Options

The client finds a set of actions that are available to them, which might move them closer to their goal.

W is for Will

From the list of options, the client selects those that they will commit to doing. (W can also stand for Wrap-up in some coaches' terminology.)

The GROW model is a general framework which cannot always be operated strictly in order, as listed here, but each element should be visited at least once.

Over time, as reality meets theory and as coaching insights arrive, goals may be revised slightly or radically – even the topic may be replaced.

TGROW can also be used in a group setting as a way of working through a situation the group, company, church or charity is facing.

A coach using a TGROW model might see the conversation develop as follows:

> You: Welcome, it's good to see you.
> Them: Thanks. You too.
> You: In the first session we often find that it's good to explore

what we will talk about. You said on the phone that you wanted to work on exploring a job change: is that correct?

Them: Yes, I have been going through the motions for a long while now. I don't think the job is going to change, and indeed there are rumours that the company may be struggling. So it may be a good time to get out.

You: OK. Well, let's talk a little about the work you do first.

Them: I am an accountant and have been since I left school.

You: Is this your first job?

Them: My second, actually. I moved to this one when my wife Katy and I moved down to London, just after we were married.

You: It was easier to move for her work?

Them: That's right, she works at the London Museum and it was much easier for me to find accountant work than for her to try and find museum work back in Sheffield.

You: So are you looking to stay in accountancy, or move away from that work?

Them: I was wondering whether that could be something we could discuss. Accountancy is all I have ever known, and it's safe. But I did wonder whether it might be time for a complete change.

You: So it sounds as if you need to decide whether to leave accountancy or not, and if you do, what job you might want?

Them: Yes.

You: What would be your aim for this session?

Them: I think it would be to talk through what my options might be. Is that realistic for our time?

You: We will see how we go.

Them: So how does this work?

You: You want to talk through your options so I am aiming to guide you to explore things. I am not here to say what those options should be, but to guide you in your thinking. Is that OK?

Them: Yes, great.

Reality

The conversation then continues by exploring the job that the coachee is doing. What they enjoy, what they don't, and what other things they enjoy in life.

Options

Under Options you might want to have a structured 'brainstorming' session. Give them time to just say all the kinds of jobs they would like.

- Are there other jobs that take their fancy?
- Would they be willing to re-train?
- How much is salary and location a consideration?
- What skills and attributes do they have?
- Have they done any psychometric tests to determine temperament or aptitude?
- What might be the next thing that they do?

Will

As a result of this conversation what do they need to do next? For example: they may need to research options further, or they may want to discuss this in more detail with their spouse. This would become a goal to be completed in readiness for the next session.

In cases where the coachee has a general sense of unease but no specific goal, it can be useful to use the wheel of life diagram.

The wheel of life diagram

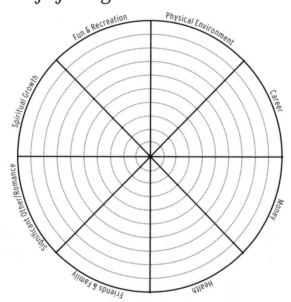

The wheel of life diagram is a simple circle with ten concentric circles within it, divided into segments. The number of segments may vary, but might be eight. You then label the circles with appropriate areas relevant to the person you are coaching.

Generic labels would be: physical environment, money, health, significant other, friends and family, spiritual growth, career, fun and recreation.

The coachee will then look at each of the categories and rate their satisfaction levels by shading in the segment of the circle. So a high satisfaction rating would be fully shaded, a less high one, partially shaded, leaving the poorest areas with very little shading, if any. This might help coachees discern which areas of life they want to focus on. They may assume they want to change jobs but discover that it's not work that's a problem, but lifestyle issues that prevent them from recovering their energy levels sufficiently to truly appreciate their work.

Is it a spiritual problem or a physical problem? They are assuming that something is wrong with their relationship with God when it's actually a physical problem making them feel low, which they interpret as being down to a spiritual cause.

There are other models used, which we will look at more briefly.

Solution-focused coaching

Many of our approaches to change are problem-focused, in that we attempt to move forward by exploring the problem: we try to understand what the problem is, what has caused it, and what we need to do to get rid of it. This works well in many situations, particularly those involving machines. For example, we may notice that our bike is not feeling very smooth to ride, which prompts us to inspect the wheels. We discover that one of the tyres is flat and so fix or replace it – problem solved! But when we are working with people, diagnosing the problem often gives us little indication of the solution and indeed may even make the situation worse!

Some counselling can sadly end up doing this. Fortunately, there is another way: we can focus on solutions instead. At heart this solution-focused approach involves:

- finding out what works and doing more of it
- stopping doing what doesn't work and doing something else

It doesn't mean that we refuse to discuss the problem but it does mean that we use any problem discussion to discover what the person wants to do, to learn about their commitment and passion, and to unearth evidence of skills and resources they are already using.

The OSKAR model

OSKAR is a framework for solution-focused coaching and once again each letter in OSKAR stands for a step in the process. It was invented by Mark McKergow with his co-author Paul Z. Jackson, for a project in the year 2000.

Outcome
What is the objective of this coaching?
What do you want to achieve today?

Scaling
On a scale of 0 to 10, with 0 representing the worst it has ever been and 10 the preferred future, where would you put the situation today?
You are at n now; what did you do to get this far?
How would you know you had got to $n+1$?

Know-how and resources
What helps you perform at n on the scale, rather than 0?
When does the outcome already happen for you – even a little bit?
What did you do to make that happen? How did you do that?

Affirm and action
What's already going well?
What is the next small step?
You are at n now, what would it take to get you to $n+1$?

Review: what's better?
What did you do that made the change happen?

What effects have the changes had?
What do you think will change next?

OSKAR has been used with profit in a business environment but could equally be employed one on one between Christians. Imagine your coachee is discouraged by their witness at work. They want to be better able to live for Christ in the workplace but they don't feel they are making progress.

Moving through the OSKAR model might go like this:

Outcome

> You: So what would you like to focus on today?
>
> Them: I was hoping to improve my witness at work.
>
> You: Where do you work?
>
> Them: At the MOD.
>
> You: OK – what would improving your witness look like?
>
> Them: Well I used to have opportunities to talk about my faith, share what I believed. Now it's dropped off. I didn't use work time for this, you understand, but had chats on breaks and occasionally over drinks after work.
>
> You: OK, so what would be a reasonable outcome to hope for?
>
> Them: Well I guess I want to be able to have at least one conversation about my faith by the end of a fortnight.
>
> You: OK.

You move next to ...

Scaling

> You: On a scale of 0 to 10, with 0 representing the worst it has ever been and 10 the preferred future, where would you put the situation today?
>
> Them: Well, I would have to say that it is around 3 now.
>
> You: So why 3?
>
> Them: Well, I guess because I used to be at an 8 or 9 earlier. I would have to say that it's a 3 because I still care about it and am looking for opportunities.

Know-how and resources

You: OK so thinking back to the 8 and 9 period, when things were working well. Why did it get to that high score?

Them: Well there was this woman who was interested in the faith: Kirsty. She used to come to church with me occasionally. She was going out with another colleague, Bill, who was more sceptical, and so we had some great chats.

You: You said 'was this woman'. What became of her?

Them: She moved away for work and we lost touch.

You: And Bill?

Them: He moved too.

Affirm and action

You: OK, so that was clearly a buoyant time for you. How did Kirsty know you were a Christian?

Them: Well, we got talking about what I had done at the weekend, so I mentioned church. I was also praying for opportunities, and for staff members.

You: Great. And so when the chance came you were ready. Do you still pray for colleagues?

Them: Yes, pretty much every day.

You: I am wondering if you are giving yourself a 3 because you don't have the same opportunities. The time with Kirsty was clearly special, but maybe you are being a little hard on yourself?

Them: Maybe. I just long to be more useful.

You: Well, let's stick with your 3. How can you move things along so that they become closer to the 8 or 9 that you enjoyed before?

Them: I will keep praying.

You: Good. What else?

Them: Well, I might try and invite other colleagues for a drink after work.

You: Are there obvious people?

Them: I guess so. There are a few who occasionally have drinks. Maybe they would come with me?

You: What effect will that have on your witness?

Them: Well, I realise my faith may not come up naturally, but it gives a chance for it to. And it will help me to get to know some people who I don't know well and pray for them.

You: Great. Can you make that into a goal?

Them: Yes, by the next time we meet – two weeks?

You: Yes.

Them: I will have invited this group for drinks after work.

You: Great. I look forward to hearing how it went.

Review (two weeks later)

You: So, how did it go?

Them: Fine, thanks.

You: Tell me about it

Them: Well, I was able to invite one of my colleagues, Gill. The people she normally goes with were away and she was happy to have a drink with me.

You: How was that?

Them: Fine. Nothing startling. She lives with her mum, who is quite active in the local council. So we talked about that. She is a keen skier and told me about a recent trip to Austria. I was able to mention church. She didn't seem too interested. But that was fine.

You: So if you had to give yourself a score. What would it be now?

Them: Well, to be honest, I feel that things are so much better, even though I didn't say anything especially Christian, I was out there and available to God. So maybe a 7 now.

You: Great, and how might this move to an 8 or 9?

Them: Well, by taking the opportunities. Maybe seeing Gill again. Keeping praying for colleagues and maybe seeing if I can spend time with other colleagues, too.

You: Excellent. Great to hear that you are so pleased.

The CLEAR Model

Another way of structuring a coaching session is the CLEAR model. The CLEAR model was developed by Peter Hawkins in the early 1980s and so pre-dates the GROW model.

CLEAR is an acronym for:

Contracting

Opening the discussion, setting the scope, establishing the desired outcomes, and agreeing the ground rules.

Listening

Using active listening, the coach helps the coachee develop their understanding of the situation and generate personal insight.

Exploring 1

Helping the coachee to understand the personal impact the situation is having on themselves.

Exploring 2

Challenging the coachee to think through possibilities for future action in resolving the situation.

Action

Supporting the coachee in choosing a way ahead and deciding the next step.

Review

Closing the intervention, reinforcing ground covered, decisions made and value added. The coach also encourages feedback from the client on what was helpful about the coaching process, what was difficult and what they would like to be different in future coaching sessions.

The CLEAR model emphasises the importance of reviewing the session. It's possible when using the GROW model to think that it's all over when we have done the Wrap-up (W). Making reviewing the coaching's effectiveness one of the basic steps, as the CLEAR model does, reinforces the value and importance of this stage.

The STOP model

Coachees sometimes have a vague inkling that something is wrong, but aren't sure what it is. Tim Gallwey, in his book *The Inner Game of Work*[1], has a process (which he calls the *tool of all tools*) called STOP. This acronym stands for:

Step back
– from action, emotion and thinking.

Think
– about what's most important.

Organise your thoughts
– to create coherence.

Proceed
– when purpose and next steps are clear.

At its centre is awareness, the ability to be fully present in the moment and to create the space in which we can choose. He believes that if STOP is the tool of all tools, awareness is the capacity of all capacities. As we have noted, awareness is a key part of making progress. We notice what we're doing, we notice the universe of possibilities of what we could be doing, and then we choose how to spend this moment in time.

Exercise

Look at the following situations and select which coaching style you would prefer to use for each:

- A teenager comes to you wanting help to find the right job.
- An electrician comes because their business has folded and they are in debt.
- A church worker is not getting on with their boss.
- A retired banker wants to use his talents for God, having taken early retirement.
- A woman's husband died a year ago and wants to 'move on'. Her children have left home and she has no ties, but isn't sure what to do.
- Someone turns up for coaching but you don't know what they want before they arrive.

[1] Tim Gallwey, *The Inner Game of Work* (London: Random House, 1999).

O5:

Setting goals

We have seen that coaching aims to provide a supportive relationship in which the coachee takes action towards the resolution of the problem or issue that they are focusing on. Most coaches find that writing down goals is of great benefit in clarifying what the coachee intends to do.

Just as the terms for coaching and mentoring lack universal definition, so it is that the word 'goals' is often confused with its cousin, 'objectives'. Some would argue that goals are deliberately broad and long-term, with objectives, concrete and specific. I recall an appraisal interview where I was at cross purposes with my boss, who used the word 'objectives' the way I used 'goals'. Thankfully we realised pretty quickly.

In this chapter we are using the word 'goals' to simply describe what we want to achieve. We will be suggesting that a vague 'goal' is unlikely to be met and that we are best served by goals if we make sure that they are SMART goals.

The SMART model

SMART stands for key things which your goals should be:
  S – Specific
  M – Measurable
  A – Attainable
  R – Realistic
  T – Time-specific

(In some lists A stands for 'action-oriented', R stands for 'relevant' and T for 'traceable'.)

As we look at each word, you will see that there is some overlap.

Specific

Comic actress, Lily Tomlin once said: 'I always wanted to be somebody, but I should have been more specific.'

Goals should be straightforward and emphasise what the coachee wants to happen. Specifics help us to focus their efforts and clearly define what they are going to do.

Specific is the *what* of the SMART model.

What are they going to do? Use action words such as: direct, organise, coordinate, lead, develop, plan, build.

Ensure the goals set are very specific, clear and easy. Instead of setting a goal to lose weight or be healthier, set a specific goal to lose 2cm off their waistline or to walk 5 miles at an aerobically challenging pace.

Measurable

If you can't measure it, you can't manage it. In the broadest sense, the whole goal statement is a measure for the project; if the goal is accomplished, then it is a success. However, there are usually several short-term or small measurements that can be built into the goal.

The coachee chooses a goal with measurable progress, so you can both see the change occur. How will they know when they reach their goal? Be specific! 'I want to read three books of 100-plus pages on my own before my birthday' shows the specific target to be measured. 'I want to be a better reader' is not as measurable.

Establish concrete criteria for measuring progress towards the attainment of each goal set. When the coachee measures their progress, they stay on track, reach their target dates, and experience the exhilaration of achievement that spurs them on to the continued effort required to reach their goals.

Attainable

The goal must be within the reach of the coachee. This means that the learning curve is not a vertical slope, that the skills needed to do the work are available, and that the project fits with the overall strategy. A realistic project will push the skills and knowledge of the coachee but it shouldn't break them. Goals set which are too far out of their reach will be de-motivating, so it's important that you work hard on setting sensible goals.

Goals that depend on someone else are not attainable and could ultimately be soul destroying. Here you need to ask, 'are there any *givens* in life, which might stop you attaining the goal?'

Attainable versus unattainable

Unattainable – I want my daughter to communicate what's going on.

Attainable – I want to create five opportunities this week when my daughter and I can spend quality time together.

The attainable/unattainable contrast is especially important when the goals involve the work of God. We may desire things that only God can do. A pastor may say that he wants to see his church 'double' in size of believers.

This is not something directly under his control. He would need to create a strategy that is in his control that he hopes will give the desired outcome. This might include increasing the training of his congregation in personal evangelism, employing staff gifted in outreach or changing the service style to appeal to outsiders.

Relevant

Is the goal being set really important to the coachee? Is this something they are doing because they feel they 'ought' to, or really want to?

Sometimes the coachee has a more 'relevant' goal which they haven't told the coach, either because they are not sure how to express it, or haven't yet opened up sufficiently.

The relevance may become clear when the coachee comes to take action. If they seem reluctant to do what they had agreed to do it may be that they have not decided on a goal that is truly relevant to them.

Time-specific

If you don't have a deadline, you don't have a goal! Set a timeframe for the goal; this might be the next time you meet. Or you may set smaller goals for the next time you meet, with the larger goal set over a longer period. For example, the goal might be to write ten job applications in the next fortnight, when the larger and major goal is get a job in the next three months. Putting an end point on the goal gives a clear target to work towards.

If you don't set a time, the commitment is too vague. It tends not to happen because the coachee feels they can start at any time. Without a time limit, there's no urgency to start taking action now. It is said that a goal without a deadline is 80 per cent less effective than one with a specific time-based deadline.

Remember, your job is to help the coachee to set SMART deadlines, but they will be goals that the coachee has agreed and set. One way of ensuring that this is so is to ask them to rate their degree of commitment to the goal. If 0 is 'not interested' and 10 is 'absolutely definitely committed', what score would you give yourself with respect to this goal? If they are not able to say 8 or above, you may need to re-visit it. If they say 6, your next question would be: 'how could we make it more likely? How could that 6 become an 8?'

Examples

You will immediately spot that the following 'goals' do not meet the SMART goals standard.

- I will improve my relationship with God
- I want a better relationship with my wife
- My time-keeping needs to get better
- I want a promotion at work
- I need to work out where I should live

These may all be legitimate desires, but the coach will work towards finding exactly what is meant by the words used, and what the coachee is willing to do to make the desire a reality. What is holding them back from this? What has been tried already? How might this be framed in SMART Goals?

So, for example, if the person believed that it would improve their relationship with God to have a daily time of Bible reading and prayer, a SMART goal might be framed thus:

By the end of the month (Time- specific) I will have developed a daily routine of 20 minutes (Measurable and Attainable) of Bible reading and prayer (Specific and Relevant to improve my relationship with God).

There may be action steps associated with this goal, perhaps including buying some Bible reading notes, getting up earlier to pray or developing a prayer list. Each of these could be framed as a SMART goal too.

Helping coachees set goals

Coaches have found it useful to explore the following areas when looking at what goals to set. You can use a grid to work through the areas.

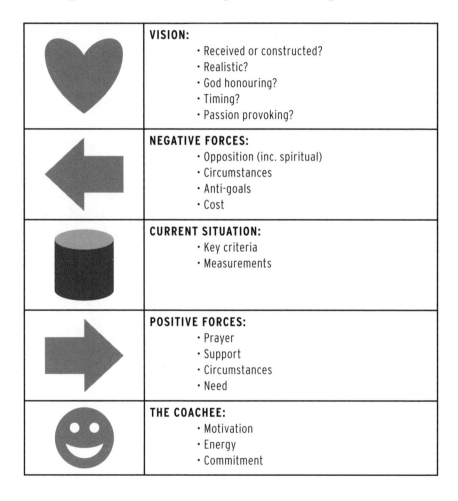

♥	**VISION:** · Received or constructed? · Realistic? · God honouring? · Timing? · Passion provoking?
←	**NEGATIVE FORCES:** · Opposition (inc. spiritual) · Circumstances · Anti-goals · Cost
▮	**CURRENT SITUATION:** · Key criteria · Measurements
→	**POSITIVE FORCES:** · Prayer · Support · Circumstances · Need
☺	**THE COACHEE:** · Motivation · Energy · Commitment

Vision

In this, we look at the extent to which the coachee has a vision for the way ahead. Is this something that they have received from others, or is it genuinely theirs? Many are stuck because they are trying to live according to others' vision and have not identified their own.

You want them to be keen to move towards their goals and if you sense there is something holding them back, it is worth investigating.

Negative forces

Sometimes there is opposition to what is being planned, from family, friends, co-workers or others. There may even be a spiritual battle.

Circumstances may seem to be working against movement. It's worth exploring whether this is providential (ie an indication of God's direction) or something to push through.

Anti-goals are those goals which we set against what we think we want to do. If a person has not done something, it may be because they secretly want the opposite more, whatever they say. It's important to address this.

Current situation

This will have been explored in the conversation, but it can also be useful to write down. Where are they now? How do they know that's where they are? How would they know they had arrived where they want to be?

Positive forces

Here we include anything that will support the process of taking action. You as coach will be a factor, but it's worth listing others as a way of encouraging the coachee.

The coachee

This is where you are looking for their enthusiasm to take the action. You support them, but the action has to come from them. You want them to be highly committed to doing the next thing. If they are not, then keep talking of re-shaping the goal until they are.

PART TWO:

Mentoring

06:

Introduction to mentoring

In the introduction to this book we noted the distinction between mentoring and coaching. Mentoring is far more directional. The mentor is typically more experienced and skilled in the matter on which the mentoree is being mentored.

A coach need know little or nothing of the topic they coach on: their job is to help the coachee to discover solutions for themselves. In mentoring, some kind of experience is necessary, whether this be in a specific area or skill, or in a more general life experience from which they will draw as they help the mentoree.

We say 'far more directional' because wise mentoring will also include a non-directional component too. The approach discussed in the coaching section is also valuable as a way of helping the mentoree imbibe the lessons imparted by the mentor.

What is mentoring?

Mentoring
An agreement, usually between two people, to meet together on a regular basis for the benefit of the mentoree.

Mentor
A person who is prepared to commit his/her time, experience and skills to help another person grow as a person in a way that is accepting, caring and beneficial to him/her. He or she is generally more experienced in the faith than the mentoree.

Mentoree

A person who invites another person to give him or her some time, support, understanding and accountability, with the aim of personal growth or the improvement of a skill, talent or task.

On his Virgin Atlantic website, Richard Branson writes of how Sir Freddie Laker was the businessperson who had the biggest influence on his early business days:

> He helped shape our vision for high-quality service at competitive prices, and was the first to bring my attention to how fiercely we would have to battle with BA to make a success of our airline. He also managed to bring great humour and a sense of fun to every situation. It was a pleasure to name one of our planes after him, as a small token of appreciation.

Many companies have mentoring programmes so that the benefits that Branson enjoyed can be known as employees value the input and experience of those further on in the field. Churches also typically have mentoring-type relationships at leadership level. Within the Church of England, ordinands will serve a three-year curacy under a vicar who will have some kind of a mentoring role (depending on the skills of the vicar, and the kind of relationship which develops). The free church has ministers helping assistants, or pastoral assistants, who are 'in training' and given a broad range of pastoral experience on which they are mentored.

TYPICAL MENTORING SITUATIONS

Mature Christian with someone younger in his/her walk with Jesus

An experienced Christian helps a new believer to know how to live the Christian life. This is typically men helping men or women helping women, and may encompass any aspect of what it means to live for Christ. It may be to counter a struggle that the Christian has faced, such as some form of addiction, release from prison or a particular area of temptation. Alternatively, it may be to enhance a perceived gifting the mentoree has.

Mature Christian with a chronologically younger Christian

The rule of thumb seems to be that an age gap of around five to ten years works best, but there is no hard and fast rule. The older the person, the greater the potential age gap that might work. It may be trickier for a 30-year-old to work with a 20-year-old, than for a 50-year-old to work with a 40-year-old.

Gifted Christian imparts their skills and approach to a novice(s) in a particular field

The areas for mentoring may include preaching, worship leading, door to door work, children's work, youth work, administration, chairing and leading meetings, catering for large numbers, managing finances or something else.

The gifted Christian shares 'good practice' with the mentoree. They may observe them in action and discuss the 'event' post-activity. In the early stages it may be a case of 'do as I do' until the mentoree becomes comfortable in developing their own style.

Peer mentoring, where two people of similar age and/ or Christian maturity agree to operate on the basis of a mentoring contract with one another

This is also simply known as 'being accountable'. This book will not focus on this kind of mentoring directly, but it can be of enormous value.

Group mentoring, where a mature Christian meets with two or three persons of similar age/Christian maturity

On occasions, this kind of mentoring may take place within a group setting, perhaps when someone with a wider ministry, who is celebrated within the field, passes on their wisdom, perhaps over a series of days. The UK Evangelist J. John and songwriter and worship leader Graham Kendrick have both mentored Christians keen to improve their preaching and worship leading. Skill is required from the mentor to ensure that equity of sharing is maintained with the mentoring group.

Infrequent mentoring – where contact is as little as every six months to a year

This kind of mentoring works when the mentor's schedule prevents regular contact but the mentoree regards infrequent contact as still valuable to them. Some people have such wise insight that even infrequent contact is deemed valuable.

Mentoring through books

Some would also include the benefit that can be derived from reading books by individuals who are prolific authors in the field in which the mentoree is interested. Some speak warmly of being mentored by those not alive, through their works. This is not the focus of this book, but important to note.

WHAT DOES A MENTOR DO?

The image of the Sherpa helping a climber to reach the summit can be helpful to describe how a mentor helps a mentoree. The Sherpa are an ethnic group from the most mountainous region of Nepal high in the Himalayas. They are regarded as elite mountaineers and experts in their local terrain, and were used by the early explorers as guides to help the ascent to many of the mountains, notably Everest, the highest mountain in the world. Sherpas have particular aptitude for work at very high altitudes, though today the term 'Sherpa' is used of the guide, regardless of their ethnic background.

There are a number of parallels between the way the Sherpa helps an explorer and a mentor helps a mentoree:

- A Sherpa has experience the climber does not have. They know the terrain and challenges.
- The Sherpa and climber 'rope up'. The rope is the climber's lifeline and connection with the Sherpa.
- A Sherpa charts an appropriate course for the climber, and knows the places that are especially awkward.
- The climber has to climb themselves. The Sherpa cannot do the climbing for them.
- If the climber gets into difficulty, the Sherpa can give particular assistance.

- When they reach the summit, the climber has the sense of accomplishment of having made it up, themselves, while at the same time, acknowledging that the Sherpa's assistance was invaluable.

The parallels are hopefully obvious. In a similar way the mentoree is assisted by the mentor to journey themselves. The mentoring contract or verbal agreement is like the rope tying the two together. The mentoree knows they have an experienced guide who leads the way and helps them keep things smooth and negotiate any difficulties.

We can summarise the kind of help provided. The mentor:

- Enhances the growth of mentoree
  This is a primary goal of any spiritual mentoring experience. The mentor's focus is the mentoree. They are asking, how can I use my expertise to ensure that the mentoree is in a better place when we complete each session together?

- Supports
  The mentor provides ongoing support as the mentoree works through the issues that are discussed. It is one thing to know what to do, quite another doing it, and the mentoring relationship provides the supportive context that helps the mentoree follow through on what they have said they will do.

- Builds a strong relationship
  There is a mutual benefit that flows from mentoring. The mentoree benefits in various ways through support, wisdom and encouragement. The mentor grows in experience, competence and personally as he/she sees God use him/her in the mentoring relationship.

- Listens
  As with coaching, mentoring does include the mentor giving attention to what the mentoree says. The mentor will speak far more than the coach typically would, but they will need to hear from the mentoree if their advice is to be pertinent.

- Offers understanding and empathy
  The mentor attempts to enter the mentoree's world; their experiences, feelings, thoughts, needs, pains, dreams, so that they can best help them.

- Models

  The mentor seeks to be an example of Christian virtues and values. If the mentoring is based on skill development then there is probably opportunity for the mentoree to see the mentor in action, demonstrating an approach that the mentor would seek to attain.

- Encourages

  The word encourage literally means, 'give courage to' and this will be part of the mentor's role as he/she urges action and praises progress made.

- Provides accountability

  The mentor provides a context for evaluating progress, measuring success and failure in reaching agreed objectives, and confessing failures, fears or weaknesses.

- Prays for the mentoree

  Prayer is not an insignificant aspect of the work. The mentor invites God to help the mentoree to accomplish God-honouring goals, and break through any hindrances that have held them back in the past.

- Speaks the truth in love (Eph. 4:15).

  Sometimes loving confrontation will be necessary to reflect back to the mentoree emotions, attitudes or behaviour that are not in keeping with spiritual, emotional or relational health.

- Provides objectivity

  A mentoree may find difficulty in seeing things differently or may ignore weaknesses, be unaware of strengths or be locked into unhelpful behaviour or thinking. The mentor may act like a mirror for the mentoree in certain situations.

- Advises

  Mentoring involves giving advice: the mentoree wants to know what to do. Advice will be given after due consideration of the needs of the mentoree and what is possible in the short and long term.

- Supports the mentoree in the attainment of desired goals

  These goals may arise out of discussion but, just as in a coaching situation, they must be 'owned' by the mentoree if they are to be implemented effectively.

WHAT CHARACTERISES A GOOD MENTORING RELATIONSHIP?

Openness and honesty

You will need to be honest with your mentoree and they will need to be honest with you. There is little point in having a mentoring relationship at all if candour is not expressed. If the purpose of the mentoring is in general life as a Christian, the mentoree needs to share their honest perception of their walk with God. If a mentor is helping a newcomer to faith, they will need to recall how they found those early days of their own conversion.

If the purpose for mentoring involves a skill or activity in which the mentor has competence, they need to honestly assess competence levels and where improvement can be made. The mentor needs to be honest with the mentoree. If a mentoring preacher only ever shares the high points of their preparation and delivery, the novice speaker might be intimidated by their mentor's apparent invincibility. It's time to search the memory banks for failings and struggles to go with any moments of breakthrough.

This degree of transparency is certainly not a given for church leaders. Many struggle to be open to those they lead: some for fear that respect may be lost, others because of a defensive outlook caused by a desire for self protection.

In his book *Mentoring: The Promise of Relational Leadership* (Paternoster, 2004), Walter Wright writes of how the late George Ladd, the professor of New Testament at Fuller Theological Seminary, Pasadena, California, and a scholar with an international reputation, mentored him. He writes:

> But George Ladd also taught me about humanness, vulnerability and the pain of life. We played handball each week and talked. I began to know a brilliant man struggling with life – a man lonely and uncertain about his legacy – a man who taught about community but found relationships difficult to sustain. He shaped forever my vision of life as community, relationships, and character but he was not a happy man himself. I began to realize that mentors do not necessarily have it all together. They are also in the process of learning and growing. They too are on

a journey. But they can still believe in you and share something of themselves with you as you walk together on your journeys.

If you are a leader and at all nervous about being vulnerable, it is worth reflecting why this is. Do you have a fear of sin being exposed? Why should that be a problem if Jesus cleanses from all sin? Do you fear others becoming aware of your failings? Is that such a big deal? Aren't we all on a journey, and doesn't grace cover us?

Mutual trust and respect

Mentoring relationships must be negotiated so that both persons are comfortable and committed. An informal preliminary meeting, for example over tea or coffee, is often a useful way to assess whether the two people should form a mentoring agreement. It is also useful to review the relationship after a few sessions. We will look at the first meeting in detail later in the book.

Friendship

Ideally mentoring is a place where laughter, mutual enjoyment of conversation and of each other's company are a feature. It helps if both parties look forward to the meeting, and there is a degree of delight in the journey.

Of course good mentoring can take place if the two do not become bosom buddies, but developing a good friendship is a good aim to have.

Belief in the mentoree

The mentor needs to gauge whether he/she sees potential in the mentoree and/or benefit in pursuing the mentoring relationship. This will provide an incentive to continue should the process occasionally become difficult. For this reason it is useful to have regular review times, so that the mentoring can be curtailed without embarrassment. This is perhaps easier when the mentoring concerns skills. It will be apparent to both people that progress is being made and the mentoree can move on to work more independently. Indeed, there will be occasions when to continue mentoring would be detrimental to what has been achieved.

Confidentiality

It is worth discussing what may or may not be shared from the mentoring relationship at the first meeting. It is often wise to put the agreement in writing for each other, though this may be deemed too formal if the mentoring relationship has arisen out of friendship. The mentor should agree not to share the mentoree's words, feelings, goals, attitudes, etc, outside the mentoring context, except with the consent of the mentoree. There would be two exceptions. As with counselling, the mentor would divulge information if the mentoree shares something that needs to be disclosed to the police, and secondly, if they believe the mentoree would be in physical or emotional danger. In these, admittedly rare cases, the mentor will explain their thinking to the mentoree. Hopefully you will not face either.

Commitment

Mentoring needs to have a high priority in the mentor's life. The time and regularity will depend on the kind of agreement that is made. This might be a short term skills based agreement, an issue-based relationship, such as dealing with finances, or a more open-ended agreement that focuses on more general matters. A mentor is wise not to take on too much, especially if they are mentoring in their own 'free' time.

Intentionality

Mentoring will not happen if plans are at all vague, or the mentoree doesn't demonstrate a willingness to meet. It's worth planning definite times, definite days/dates and a definite place to meet. If necessary, send reminders via text or email ahead of time. There should be that sense that there are few more important meetings that will happen that week.

Patience

Mentoring typically involves change of some sort, and most of us find that change takes time. It is often a case of three steps forward, two steps back and mentors are wise to recall their slowness to grasp the issues in hand, and implement the changes necessary. It is not enough for a mentor to know what needs to be done. Their emotional support is vital.

Boundaries

Don't assume that the mentoree understands what you are doing, especially early on. Be very clear about what you are offering and the kind of relationship that exists outside the regular meeting. If the mentor and mentoree have an existing friendship then it may seem odd for limits to be suddenly set concerning when contact can be made, but it is a good principle for all involved in one to one helping to be careful to set appropriate boundaries. Some caring relationships have unravelled when the person caring has been swamped by the demands of the person being helped. You will have a sense of what will be appropriate, but it's worth erring on the side of caution.

WHO SHOULD CONSIDER BECOMING A MENTOR?

At this point you may well be thinking, 'should I mentor people or not?' Ideally, the following needs to be true:

You are a maturing Christian willing to grow in your faith

Mentoring is not an activity for someone 'who is a novice themselves' but someone who has a buoyant walk with God and a desire to help others. So you would have a good reputation within the local church as a faithful and stable believer and be active in service in some area, either in the church or the wider community.

You want to help others grow

Every mentor wants to see others flourish, either in the skill or area of expertise, or in Christian life in general. Not every highly gifted person has the heart and desire to see others move on, and not every highly gifted person has learned the skills necessary to impart what they know to others. Some seem to have what we might call an 'instinctive' way of serving. They are incapable of imparting what they do to others because frankly they do not really know what they do! This is especially true of some entrepreneurial leaders who are blessed with a capacity to lead without being quite sure why they do it the way they do.

You are willing to commit regular time to another person

The first two qualities may be in place, but if you are too busy, then don't do it until you can free up the time. You may have the kind of skills and insights that means that mentorees will flock to benefit from you at intermittent intervals, but don't bank on it! Most of us need to give a regular, weekly, or fortnightly time to a mentoree, and do so when we are at our best, not when we are exhausted and troubled by other demands.

You are keen to equip yourself to be the best you can be for other Christians

A good mentor is willing to serve others by providing their expertise and experience and also by learning and growing so they may better serve. You can always improve. There are books to read, courses to take, insights to enjoy.

You have a skill or area of expertise in which another believer wishes to grow

Clearly mentors that offer their services in an expertise need to have a recognised gifting in the setting in which the service is offered. This may be with a local church or wider afield. Self awareness is important in this regard. Romans 12:3 says: 'do not think of yourself more highly than you ought, but rather think of yourself with sober judgment, in accordance with the faith God has distributed to each of you.' You will know whether you have an area of service in which others are regularly edified. If you are unsure, you are wise to talk with those who know you well and would tell you straight.

WHO SHOULD MENTOR WHOM?

In general, mentoring for spiritual growth is going to be male to male or female to female. This can more easily facilitate the kind of sharing that will enable understanding to take place and guards both parties against emotional involvement.

However, when mentoring is skills based, then there is more latitude, especially when the schedule of meetings is of short duration. If it is male–female then wisdom is exercised on where the conversation takes place, so that both parties feel comfortable. It may be best to meet in a public place, if that's possible.

Walter Wright has written of the considerable help he has received from female mentors. He acknowledges the dangers of emotional involvement, but feels that providing appropriate boundaries are in place, there should be no restriction. In his case, his wife met the mentor and was comfortable with the work they were doing. Each case needs to be taken on its own merits.

FOR HOW LONG WILL YOUR MENTORING AGREEMENT LAST?

If mentoring is for personal growth, six months would be a minimum in normal circumstances. A year could prove more beneficial. A skills/knowledge-based focus might be shorter. Whatever the length of time decided, it should be a fixed time limit, agreed to by both persons involved. Open-ended arrangements are hard to change if the mentoring is not working out for either person. It would be better to arrange for a short period that can be extended, then reassess the mentoring relationship during the second-to-last meeting. At this time you may discuss whether it will continue or not and provide opportunity for an effective closure during the last session, if necessary. If the mentoring arrangement works well and both people are in agreement, it may be continued for another agreed period of time.

HOW MIGHT A MENTORING RELATIONSHIP BE ARRANGED?

- In church settings where there is a culture and understanding around what mentoring (and indeed coaching) is, mentoring relationships may develop quite easily.
- A Christian leader or friend may suggest that someone finds a mentor, as a way of focusing on a developmental need.
- It may be part of the way the church develops newcomers to the faith.
- It may be initiated by either the mentoree or, occasionally, by the mentor.
- It may be developed from mutual interests (eg in an area of ministry). Many more experienced in an area long to pass on their expertise to those who need their help.
- The mentor advertises their role via a website, church notice board, church newsletter or similar.

You may feel you want mentoring to become a major part of your life: maybe this would become a part-time or full-time job, maybe you are retired and able to give time to it. A website can attract clients, and well placed 'ads' let people know you can be approached.

07:

The Bible and mentoring

Coaching and mentoring are increasingly valued and recognised within the Christian community. But there are still those who question their value. Various objections are offered, including the belief that all we really need are the Bible and prayer. Our contention in this book is that prayer and Bible reading are enhanced by good mentoring and that there are places where the Bible itself encourages the very approaches that mentoring advocates.

Christians ask for a mentor because they need:

- To have someone who is willing to spend time with them and to listen to them
- To see their questions and issues from another point of view
- To have someone who is willing to be there for them
- To explore better ways of handling their problems
- To learn from a mentor's skill and expertise
- To be held accountable for their journey towards Christian maturity

God's involved!

It's clear that a fundamental difference between Christian mentoring and mentoring in other areas, such as business, sport or public speaking, is the involvement of God in the process. We do not have to rely on our own strength in mentoring – we have the perfect Counsellor, 'the one called alongside to help' (1 John 2:1, NASB, footnote).

Remember Jesus' words to His disciples:

> If you love me, keep my commands. And I will ask the Father, and he will give you another advocate to help you and be with you for ever – the Spirit of truth. The world cannot accept him, because it neither sees him nor knows him. But you know him, for he lives with you and will be in you. I will not leave you as orphans; I will come to you. (John 14:15–18)

> But very truly I tell you, it is for your good that I am going away. Unless I go away, the Advocate will not come to you; but if I go, I will send him to you. (John 16:7)

The Holy Spirit lives within us. We are prayerful before, during and after the mentoring session, that we may sense His direction and pick up on any cues that He gives. The Holy Spirit is 'the mentor supreme'. Just as you would not want to interfere in the life of a married couple because you know that they have a special and necessarily private bond, so you are wise to be careful not to violate what the Holy Spirit is doing within a believer's life, but rather support it.

The Bible

> All Scripture is God-breathed and is useful for teaching, rebuking, correcting and training in righteousness, so that the servant of God may be thoroughly equipped for every good work. (2 Tim. 3:16–17)

The Bible is a vital tool for personal preparation – as we understand the love and grace of God for us, we can be more positive and more effective in helping others.

As we have noted already in Chapter 1, it provides foundational truths about the human condition which provide a context for all our work. On occasions we may choose to share Bible insights with the mentoree in a relaxed way as part of the conversation. In certain situations a short passage from the Bible, written out, may be helpful to leave with your mentoree for encouragement or advice.

Dynamic biblical relationships

To those who question whether mentoring is 'biblical' we can point to the following examples. None will exactly mirror the kind of mentoring relationships you may have, but all give a hint that the one to one work you are engaged in is thoroughly in line with the way God has worked in the past and works today.

Jethro and Moses

The next day Moses took his seat to serve as judge for the people, and they stood round him from morning till evening. When his father-in-law saw all that Moses was doing for the people, he said, 'What is this you are doing for the people? Why do you alone sit as judge, while all these people stand round you from morning till evening?'

Moses answered him, 'Because the people come to me to seek God's will. Whenever they have a dispute, it is brought to me, and I decide between the parties and inform them of God's decrees and instructions.'

Moses' father-in-law replied, 'What you are doing is not good. You and these people who come to you will only wear yourselves out. The work is too heavy for you; you cannot handle it alone. Listen now to me and I will give you some advice, and may God be with you. You must be the people's representative before God and bring their disputes to him. Teach them his decrees and instructions, and show them the way they are to live and how they are to behave. But select capable men from all the people – men who fear God, trustworthy men who hate dishonest gain – and appoint them as officials over thousands, hundreds, fifties and tens. Let them serve as judges for the people at all times, but let them bring every difficult case to you; the simple cases they can decide themselves. That will make your load lighter, because they will share it with you. If you do this and God so commands, you will be able to stand the strain, and all these people will go home satisfied.'

Moses listened to his father-in-law and did everything he said. He chose capable men from all Israel and made them leaders of the people, officials over thousands, hundreds, fifties and tens.

> They served as judges for the people at all times. The difficult
> cases they brought to Moses, but the simple ones they decided
> themselves.
> Then Moses sent his father-in-law on his way, and Jethro returned
> to his own country.
> (Exod. 18:13–27)

In this passage, Jethro, Moses' father-in–law, noted the way in which
Moses was working and invited himself into a mentoring relationship of
sorts. He was detached from the activity, so he was able to see what was
going on. Moses was working all day giving judgments to the people. It
was like a doctors' surgery, but with only one doctor. Jethro observed it
was exhausting for Moses and meant some may spend all day standing in
line. He advised that Moses choose and appoint appropriate officials who
can ease the burden. They would oversee groups of thousands, hundreds,
fifties and tens, and tend to deal with the easier matters. Moses could then
handle the more challenging cases, thus making better use of his time.

Lesson

We learn that it is important to give advice when we feel it's appropriate
– but we do so with grace, as Jethro did. Note especially verse 19: 'Listen
now to me and I will give you some advice, and may God be with you.'
Jethro is giving advice, but acknowledging the need for God to be in the
process if it is to succeed.

Moses and Joshua

> At that time I commanded Joshua: 'You have seen with your own
> eyes all that the LORD your God has done to these two kings.
> The LORD will do the same to all the kingdoms over there where
> you are going. Do not be afraid of them; the LORD your God
> himself will fight for you.'
> At that time I pleaded with the LORD: 'Sovereign LORD, you have
> begun to show to your servant your greatness and your strong
> hand. For what god is there in heaven or on earth who can do the
> deeds and mighty works you do? Let me go over and see the good
> land beyond the Jordan – that fine hill country and Lebanon.'
> But because of you the LORD was angry with me and would not

listen to me. 'That is enough,' the LORD said. 'Do not speak to me any more about this matter. Go up to the top of Pisgah and look west and north and south and east. Look at the land with your own eyes, since you are not going to cross this Jordan. But commission Joshua, and encourage and strengthen him, for he will lead this people across and will cause them to inherit the land that you will see.' So we stayed in the valley near Beth Peor. (Deut 3:21–29).

Moses came with Joshua son of Nun and spoke all the words of this song in the hearing of the people. When Moses had finished reciting all these words to all Israel, he said to them, 'Take to heart all the words I have solemnly declared to you this day, so that you may command your children to obey carefully all the words of this law. They are not just idle words for you – they are your life. By them you will live long in the land you are crossing the Jordan to possess.' (Deut. 32:44–47)

Now Joshua son of Nun was filled with the spirit of wisdom because Moses had laid his hands on him. So the Israelites listened to him and did what the LORD had commanded Moses. (Deut 34:9)

The relationship between Moses and Joshua was very different from that of Moses and Jethro, though it would be good to think that Moses learned from how his father-in-law advised him. Moses handed over the leadership of Israel to Joshua at the Lord's command. We are told that Joshua is filled with the Spirit of wisdom because Moses had laid his hands upon him. But you can be sure that Joshua had observed Moses' leadership and was able to learn from Moses what leading Israel would mean. We are specifically told that Moses addressed the people in Deut 31:7 so that they knew Joshua had his blessing. Joshua had big sandals to fill.

Lesson
God may look for us to mentor someone who will succeed us in the role we currently occupy. There will be a degree of observation as well as conversation within this kind of mentoring.

Elijah and Elisha

> He replied, 'I have been very zealous for the LORD God
> Almighty. The Israelites have rejected your covenant, torn down
> your altars, and put your prophets to death with the sword. I am
> the only one left, and now they are trying to kill me too.'
> The LORD said to him, 'Go back the way you came, and go to
> the Desert of Damascus. When you get there, anoint Hazael king
> over Aram. Also, anoint Jehu son of Nimshi king over Israel, and
> anoint Elisha son of Shaphat from Abel Meholah to succeed you
> as prophet. Jehu will put to death any who escape the sword of
> Hazael, and Elisha will put to death any who escape the sword of
> Jehu. Yet I reserve seven thousand in Israel – all whose knees have
> not bowed down to Baal and whose mouths have not kissed him.'
> (1 Kings 19:14–18)

> When they had crossed, Elijah said to Elisha, 'Tell me, what can
> I do for you before I am taken from you?'
> 'Let me inherit a double portion of your spirit,' Elisha replied.
> 'You have asked a difficult thing,' Elijah said, 'yet if you see me
> when I am taken from you, it will be yours – otherwise, it will not.'
> As they were walking along and talking together, suddenly a
> chariot of fire and horses of fire appeared and separated the two
> of them, and Elijah went up to heaven in a whirlwind. Elisha
> saw this and cried out, 'My father! My father! The chariots and
> horsemen of Israel!' And Elisha saw him no more. Then he took
> hold of his garment and tore it in two.
> Elisha then picked up Elijah's cloak that had fallen from him and
> went back and stood on the bank of the Jordan. He took the cloak
> that had fallen from Elijah and struck the water with it. 'Where
> now is the LORD, the God of Elijah?' he asked. When he struck the
> water, it divided to the right and to the left, and he crossed over.
> (2 Kings 2:9–14)

There are similarities between Elijah and Elisha as between Moses
and Joshua. In both cases the 'mentoree' took on the role that the
mentor had occupied. But in the case of Elijah and Elisha there was
a considerable period of overlap. Elisha is aware that he is the heir

apparent and requests that he receive a double portion of the anointing that Elijah has received.

Lesson

Elisha would have observed Elijah at work and no doubt reflected on how his prophecies were received. Mentoring may include a lot of observation of what is done as well as conversation about it. You may have formal times when you chat, but it's also useful to have opportunities where your mentoree observes you in action, especially if your mentoring is skills-based.

Barnabas and Saul

When he came to Jerusalem, he tried to join the disciples, but they were all afraid of him, not believing that he really was a disciple. But Barnabas took him and brought him to the apostles. He told them how Saul on his journey had seen the Lord and that the Lord had spoken to him, and how in Damascus he had preached fearlessly in the name of Jesus. So Saul stayed with them and moved about freely in Jerusalem, speaking boldly in the name of the Lord. He talked and debated with the Hellenistic Jews, but they tried to kill him. When the believers learned of this, they took him down to Caesarea and sent him off to Tarsus. Then the church throughout Judea, Galilee and Samaria enjoyed a time of peace and was strengthened. Living in the fear of the Lord and encouraged by the Holy Spirit, it increased in numbers. (Acts 9:26–31)

News of this reached the church in Jerusalem, and they sent Barnabas to Antioch. When he arrived and saw what the grace of God had done, he was glad and encouraged them all to remain true to the Lord with all their hearts. He was a good man, full of the Holy Spirit and faith, and a great number of people were brought to the Lord.
Then Barnabas went to Tarsus to look for Saul, and when he found him, he brought him to Antioch. So for a whole year Barnabas and Saul met with the church and taught great numbers of people. The disciples were called Christians first at Antioch. (Acts 11:22–26)

Barnabas has a significant and often overlooked role in the Early Church. His befriending of the apostle Paul in the early days of his conversion led to Paul's acceptance by the other apostles in Jerusalem. When Paul had returned to his home town of Tarsus it was Barnabas who travelled to encourage him to leave to help the church in Antioch. At Antioch, God indicated that Paul and Barnabas were to be mission partners and the rest, as they say, is history.

Lesson

In this case the 'mentoring' was short-term and for a particular purpose at the start of Paul's ministry. Sometimes our mentoring will be the same: we come alongside someone to help them through a particular patch.

Barnabas and John Mark

> When Barnabas and Saul had finished their mission, they returned from Jerusalem, taking with them John, also called Mark. (Acts 12:25)

> Some time later Paul said to Barnabas, 'Let us go back and visit the believers in all the towns where we preached the word of the Lord and see how they are doing.' Barnabas wanted to take John, also called Mark, with them, but Paul did not think it wise to take him, because he had deserted them in Pamphylia and had not continued with them in the work. They had such a sharp disagreement that they parted company. Barnabas took Mark and sailed for Cyprus, but Paul chose Silas and left, commended by the believers to the grace of the Lord. He went through Syria and Cilicia, strengthening the churches. (Acts 15:36–41)

Barnabas exercised his gracious nature towards John Mark and ended up falling out with Paul over it. John Mark had backed out of a mission trip, much to Paul's annoyance, and when the time came to pick sides to take on the next trip John Mark was dropped. Barnabas stuck up for him and split with Paul. John Mark went on to write the Gospel of Mark.

Lesson

Sometimes it will be necessary to mentor someone who has failed in some way in the past. In Mark's case, Barnabas' help would help him stay focused, and in due course, Mark's Gospel is the result: not a bad outcome!

Paul, Timothy and Titus

> Command and teach these things. Don't let anyone look down on you because you are young, but set an example for the believers in speech, in conduct, in love, in faith and in purity. Until I come, devote yourself to the public reading of Scripture, to preaching and to teaching. Do not neglect your gift, which was given you through prophecy when the body of elders laid their hands on you. (1 Tim. 4:11–14)

> You, however, know all about my teaching, my way of life, my purpose, faith, patience, love, endurance, persecutions, sufferings – what kinds of things happened to me in Antioch, Iconium and Lystra, the persecutions I endured. Yet the Lord rescued me from all of them. In fact, everyone who wants to live a godly life in Christ Jesus will be persecuted, while evildoers and impostors will go from bad to worse, deceiving and being deceived. But as for you, continue in what you have learned and have become convinced of, because you know those from whom you learned it, and how from infancy you have known the Holy Scriptures, which are able to make you wise for salvation through faith in Christ Jesus. (2 Tim. 3:10–15)

> You, however, must teach what is appropriate to sound doctrine. Teach the older men to be temperate, worthy of respect, self-controlled, and sound in faith, in love and in endurance.
> Likewise, teach the older women to be reverent in the way they live, not to be slanderers or addicted to much wine, but to teach what is good. Then they can urge the younger women to love their husbands and children, to be self-controlled and pure, to be busy at home, to be kind, and to be subject to their husbands, so that no one will malign the word of God.

> Similarly, encourage the young men to be self-controlled. In everything set them an example by doing what is good. In your teaching show integrity, seriousness and soundness of speech that cannot be condemned, so that those who oppose you may be ashamed because they have nothing bad to say about us ...
> These, then, are the things you should teach. Encourage and rebuke with all authority. Do not let anyone despise you. (Titus 2:1-8, 15)

The letters of Titus, 1 and 2 Timothy are called the pastoral epistles by some. In fact, Titus and Timothy were effectively apostolic emissaries sent by Paul to help establish churches in Crete and Ephesus. The letters themselves reflect the heartfelt concern of the apostle for his younger friends, whom he had trusted to work in tough church situations. The letters are full of advice and warning to these two relative novices.

Lesson

Sometimes our mentoring will be supporting people as they function very competently within their role. Paul clearly trusts Titus and Timothy or he wouldn't have sent them. But he does know he needs to encourage them and advise them. The letters are like 'mentoring documents' giving us some of Paul's best advice for his friends as they faced tough times. Paul also reveals something of his own heart as he encourages them.

You can be confident that the Spirit of God will come alongside to help if you invite Him. Your role ultimately is to help the other person grow further towards maturity as a lover and follower of Jesus Christ.

Knowing your limits

Mentoring is not a poor imitation of counselling. You are not the rescuer – mentoring is not a counselling arrangement. You need to think carefully about what you can offer. If you are mentoring someone to improve efficiency in a task, which areas are you competent in? When you don't know, say so. You don't have to have it 'all together', or know everything about the Bible. When you are out of your depth, seek outside help. It is better to be upfront when you are uncertain about what is the correct path forward. It is worth having a list of people whom you know you can call. Your mentoring responsibilities are limited to what you agree on in the mentoring covenant. Take care that you do not promise more than you are able to deliver!

That said, don't bail out too soon. God may equip you in the moment to do more than you could have imagined. Remember, prayer support is one of the most significant functions of a spiritual mentor.

Your personal resources for mentoring

As you have been reading this book you may already have an idea of whether you should coach, or mentor, or do both or neither! Below is a list of questions that will help you in your further assessment. Sometimes we are the worst at assessing ourselves so you may want to see what a few of your friends and family think as well.

Below are listed some personal resources that a mentor may, potentially, bring to a mentoring relationship:

1. Read through the resources listed and, in the vacant lines, add any others that you believe should be included.
2. Identify **three** of these resources that you believe are your current primary strength areas. Place an 'S' for Strengths in the boxes next to these.
3. Identify **no more than three** areas that you perceive are currently growth areas for you. Write 'GA' for Growth Areas in the box(es) next to these.

Personal resources – Strengths and Growth Areas

☐ God's heart to see others come to know Him better

☐ The empowering of the Holy Spirit for ministry

☐ The fruit of the Spirit (Galatians 5:22–23)

☐ Specific spiritual gifts

☐ Effectiveness in particular ministry areas, now or in the past

☐ Failure in particular ministry areas (which has produced significant learning)

☐ A unique life story and life experience

☐ Lessons learnt from life, and from serving God

☐ A teachable heart to discover and address untapped potential or weaknesses

☐ Things you enjoy doing and do well

☐ Particular skills and life experience in which you have proved yourself competent

....

....

....

....

....

Action

Reflect on your self-assessment above. Has this helped you focus on whether you want to be a mentor? Has it helped decide the kind of mentoring you could do?

08:

The mentoring meeting

We have looked at mentoring in general and at the way the Bible supports the idea. We turn next to look at a typical mentoring meeting. What happens?

Decide what you will focus on

If your mentoring is focusing on an area of skill then it may be obvious what you will be focusing on, but if you mentor people in life matters then the mentoree will benefit from a self-inventory. This inventory would aim to provide a holistic overview of how the mentoree is travelling in life.

As a mentor, you will come to understand better the unique person with whom you are relating, and become more aware of the characteristics that may either accelerate or slow down personal growth.

Possible areas for self-evaluation:

- Character issues such as integrity, reliability, responsibility
- Personal values
- Significant life events and experiences (positive and negative)
- Personality issues
- Spiritual life, growth and health
- Physical and emotional wellbeing
- Relationship and social issues
- Education and employment
- Lifestyle issues
- Communication and conflict styles

- Successes and failures
- Dreams and desires
- Finances and material possessions
- Growing as a person:
  - Building good family relationships – spouse, children, parents; building good relationships with people in general
  - Managing sexual relationships well
  - Coping with singleness
  - Handling grief and disappointment

You may revise the topic if other more important ones emerge in the mentoring process.

As you discuss how the mentoree wants to change, these broad areas will be given more specific goals – for example, resolving conflict might become: 'In the next fortnight I will have phoned the person I am in conflict with to arrange a meeting where I will share how I feel and ask to hear their point of view, with a view to reaching mutual understanding.'

Under the coaching section we looked at making SMART goals (Chapter 5). You may want to remind yourself of these.

Exercise
Look at the areas above and evaluate your own present 'state of wellbeing', using the self-evaluation categories above.

Rank each item from 0–5, with 0 being *no concerns* through to 5 being *a major challenge for me at present.*

Setting godly goals in a mentoring relationship

The self-inventory can help the mentoree decide what they want to focus on.

Goal setting in mentoring has many similarities with coaching. We should avoid imposing our own goals on the mentoree, otherwise the mentoree will not truly 'own' them. Nevertheless, if we are looking at an area where the mentoree is looking to improve a skill, you may want to suggest a goal initially as you may have a better idea about what may be possible. But do make sure that they agree the goal themselves, and if you are in any doubt ask them to state the goal that they believe they can meet.

Remember that you are aiming for SMART goals (goals that are: specific, measurable, attainable, relevant and time-specific). Note that it may take a couple of sessions before you settle on what you both want in this contract, and before the mentoree can formulate his or her goals. Be patient!

Establish a mentoring contract

In the first meeting you will establish what kind of mentoring you are planning. You will underline the timeframe, boundaries and expectations. If you charge for mentoring you will make the financial side clear and clarify when you want to be paid and how. It is good practice to have a signed agreement, but you will need to take a view on whether this is appropriate in your context or not.

Things to agree:
- When will you meet?

  Agree together on the best time to meet, for both of you, not just the mentoree. If you prefer a relaxed environment, consider meeting for breakfast or tea or coffee, or during a work lunch break.
- Where will you meet?

  Wherever you meet, ensure that you are both comfortable and able to share and pray freely. If you mentor someone of the opposite sex, it may be preferable in a public place or church setting where others are in close proximity.
- How often will you meet?

  You might choose to meet weekly, fortnightly, monthly or less frequently. As a guide, the longer the period of commitment, the longer the time gaps between meetings can be without weakening the mentoring process. However, if the time gaps are too long, the impact of mentoring may be weakened. Each situation needs to be discussed on its own merits.
- How long will each session last?

  A session of 45 to 90 minutes might be suitable, but there are no rigid rules here. The longer the meeting, the better the possibility of achieving a good relationship. At the same time, it is important not to spend too long – time may be wasted or both parties become weary and the value is then reduced.

• How long will you continue meeting before re-evaluating?
It's wise to review after a few sessions, then after three months – you can then re-negotiate for a further three months rather than be caught in a relationship that may not be working.

• What else should you agree upon?
– The place of phone conversations/informal contact between sessions.
– The importance of honest and open sharing.
– Commitment by the mentor to pray for the mentoree.
– Commitment by the mentoree to be held accountable, especially in the areas agreed upon in his or her goals for this mentoring relationship.

Some suggestions for the first meeting

• Meet informally at first – perhaps chat together over a meal or coffee.
• Prepare yourself to be warm and positive. The first meeting is very important!
• Don't expect too much. You will take time to get to know each other.
• Share a little about yourself and why you want to be (or are) a mentor.
• Invite the other person to share anything he/she wants to about his/her life history, including concerns, hopes, dreams, fears, etc. This could take up most of the time in the first meeting. Remember, for some people, just being heard is important.
• Make a mental note of any important facts. Write them down later and keep your notes in a safe place. Names of people close to them are especially important.
• Discuss what you both expect, and what you are willing to do and not do.

- Begin to formulate your mentoring contract.
- Remember that your role as a mentor is to:
  - Listen – this is one of the most important things to do.
  - Attend – show your interest and desire to understand what is occurring in the life of the mentoree.
  - Observe – body language, facial expressions, mood, changes from usual personality.
  - Ask questions that will assist the mentoree to search successfully for godly answers to his/her life issues.
- Share insights and experiences that may be relevant to the mentoree – but take care not to dominate.
- Advise – make suggestions, if you believe you can.
- Encourage.
- Inform of helpful resources (when needed). Refer to a more expert person (when needed).
- Pray.
- Follow up.

Some suggestions for subsequent meetings

- Confirm appointments one week ahead. Be reliable – turn up on time!
- First impressions are important. Be warm but don't put it on. If you have had a bad week, say so at an appropriate time.
- Review key points from the last meeting as a link into the current meeting.
- Share anything that God has been showing you that will encourage the mentoree.
- Remember to listen as much as you talk. Plan for more questions than answers. Guide the mentoree in his/her own journey of exploration.
- Check where your mentoree is at – 'What's been happening since we last met?'
- Hold your mentoree accountable – 'How have you been going with the things we talked about last time?'

- Check for further issues – 'Is there anything else you want to talk about today?'
- Use questions to guide discussion of any issues raised.
- Explore options as the person decides what he/she should do.
- Encourage the person to commit to his/her chosen approach.
- Take time briefly to share anything you believe may be helpful.
- Pray together as and when appropriate.

After you meet

- Rewrite any notes you may have jotted down in the session wherever you plan to keep brief notes about each mentoree. Use a code and keep notes safe to preserve confidentiality. Highlight any tasks you have committed yourself to do on their behalf, such as writing an exercise, finding a book and so on.
- 'Close the file' mentally, emotionally and spiritually afterwards, giving it over to God and trusting the person's ongoing growth to Him.
- Be friendly when you see your mentoree in situations other than that of mentoring. If not, the relationship will appear superficial.
- Seek wisdom from God to guide and shape your next meeting.

Questions to consider

Things to think through

Take some time before God to think and pray about the questions below. If you are not formally mentoring at present, these may help you assess how you feel about beginning to mentor at this stage.

If you are already mentoring, take time to reassess your mentoring relationship(s) in the light of these questions:

- What do you see as the advantages of a more formal approach to mentoring? Are there any disadvantages? If so, what would they be?

- What priority does God want mentoring to have in my life at present?
- How willing am I to invest quality time in a mentoree?
- What sort of a mentoring relationship am I comfortable with?
- What length of time should I commit to this relationship?
- Am I happy to share more than my time with my mentoree – resources such as books, DVDs or CDs?
- What will I do if my mentoree is consistently late or misses appointments?
- Am I prepared to confront and challenge my mentoree, if necessary?
- How open and transparent am I prepared to be with my mentoree?

A HEALTHY ENDING

There needs to be a definite end to a mentoring relationship, otherwise both parties are left dissatisfied. Even if a mentoring relationship does not work out well, it is better to try to meet one final time and have closure.

If you plan to end a mentoring relationship, work towards this during your last three sessions together. This helps to handle any grief involved.

In closing, look at the mentoree's goals and evaluate what has been achieved. Both of you need to evaluate the whole mentoring experience.

Celebrate the relationship, perhaps with special food or maybe a gift to each other!

If you are in the same church, talk about where your relationship will go from here. Often you still stay close friends, but just won't be meeting formally.

Realise there may be grief involved in this closure, so be gentle with yourself!

09:

Questions and answers in a mentoring context

The role of questions and answers has some similarity with what we looked at within the coaching process. You will need to listen carefully if you are to pick up on what is key to the mentoree and your questions will help to develop the conversation, but you will be far more directive than you would be in coaching. You may provide answers or solutions. Nevertheless, questions are equally important within the mentoring process.

What makes a good question?

It engages your mentoree – it is interesting to him/her
You won't know what to ask or where to head without having first explored the issues to be discussed in the preliminary work already considered. You will have a good idea of what to say once you have discussed where they want to head and what they want to achieve.

It is relevant to what has been said
You may have an agenda in terms of where you think you are heading, but you need to pay attention to everything they say, even if it seems irrelevant. 'Why do you say that?' or 'why do you think that?' are great questions to ask if you think that you are getting off track at all. Sometimes they will give you important insights.

It is helpful, not distracting

Good questions are focused on the matter in hand. Once you have done your ground work in looking at the broader issues, you will need to stay focused. Time is precious and you are wise to only ask those questions you believe helpful to achieving your goal. Of course, if your mentoring is focused upon general matters over the long term then you can afford to be more wide-ranging, but you don't want the sessions to descend into mere unfocused chit chat as may be enjoyed at the pub. Your role is to help the mentoree reflect and assess their life so that they can make progress where they believe they should.

It is clear and as simple as possible

Long and rambling questions are no help. Your questions do not need to parade your knowledge, there will be plenty of time for that. You can direct the mentoree with short and simple questions based around the 'who, what, where, when, and why' questions beloved of journalists.

How often have you done that? Why did you do it that way? What was in your mind when you did that?

It encourages thoughtfulness, not a 'yes/no' answer

We noted when looking at coaching that closed-ended questions fail to move things forward. We strive for open-ended questions that help the mentoree explore their life.

What good questions do

They clarify

Sometimes mentors need to ask questions simply to clarify what the mentoree is sharing, particularly if he or she is upset or worried over a situation. You can also ask questions that will clarify things for the mentoree, by reflecting back what he or she is conveying non-verbally and by re-stating what has been shared. 'You said things were okay, but you looked sad. What are you really feeling?' 'You seem to be unsure what to do. Is that right?'

They open up new possibilities
'Are there other possible ways of dealing with this situation/problem?'
'Is there someone around who could help you in this situation?'

They invite exploration
'Have you asked yourself what you *want* when you do that?' 'What may happen if you do that?' 'What do you *think* when that happens?'

They help your mentoree to think differently
'What would be different if this problem went away now?' 'There are some things in this that you can't change. What could you change?'

They probe
'This seems to be very painful for you, could you tell me more?' 'Am I right in thinking you are upset about that?' 'What may be the positive and negative results if you do that?'

They enable your mentoree to reflect
'How do you feel as you recall what happened for you?' 'What can you learn from this experience?' 'What things, if any, would you do differently next time?'

Using questions wisely

- Don't ask too many questions.
- Wait until the other person has an opportunity to think and reply fully, before you consider asking another question.
- Don't be too personal with your questions. None of us like to feel our private space is being invaded without our invitation.
- Be gentle. Always give your mentoree an 'out' in case he or she does not wish to answer. Remember, a non-threatening atmosphere develops trust.

Listening

In our look at coaching we noted how important listening is to the process. Listening becomes the basis upon which the coach helps the coachee discover the answers to the issues they are facing.

Listening is no less important in mentoring, and you are wise to use the non-judgmental approach advocated in a coaching setting. Your role is far more directional and you might expect to do far more talking and answering of their questions, but you will still need to take the lead and set the agenda.

Learning to 'listen' with more than our ears

People tend to judge our true meaning by what they see more than what they hear. Our body language, gestures, tone of voice and facial expressions are very important communication tools. Often these strengthen what we say, as when a person says: 'I'm really angry!' and thumps the table to prove it.

Conversely, sometimes what a person says is contradicted by what his/her body language, expressions, tone and gestures are communicating. For example, if a person says, 'I'm not angry!' but looks absolutely furious, what do you believe?

Therefore, it is best to discern the 'presence' of your mentoree when he or she first arrives. How does he/she appear? What is his/her mood? Is he/she quiet or talkative, calm or agitated, etc? Do your mentoree's spoken words conflict with his or her expression, posture, tone, and other signals? For example, they may say they are fine, but their facial expression portrays something rather different. What does this mean? What are they really communicating?

Ask yourself: 'What is the person really saying?' This is where you weigh up the other communication tools as well as the words that are being used. This provides the deeper communication picture.

Learning to pay attention

Use your body language and facial expressions as well as words to express your interest. Use your expressions and nods of the head to demonstrate that you understand and are 'tracking' with him/her. Really listen to the words, being careful not to jump to conclusions.

Learning to 'feed back'

Listen well so that you can repeat accurately the heart of what has been spoken, and so that you can re-state what the other person has said in your own words.

Learning to 'clarify'

Use questions and comments to make sure you understand what your mentoree is really trying to say. Sensitively reflect back what is being conveyed both verbally and non-verbally.

Learning to show 'empathy'

Empathy is the art of 'walking in another person's shoes' without trying to carry his or her load. It involves showing support without becoming emotionally enmeshed in your mentoree's issues. Try to be aware of what is happening emotionally for you personally as your mentoree shares, and to engage with objectivity. Use empathy to demonstrate care, acceptance and understanding.

Invite the Holy Spirit, the 'Comforter', to make known what the key issues are, and the appropriate processes with which to face and address them.

Learn to be aware of how our own opinion/experience/mental pictures/memories can interfere with good communication.

Learning to be silent

Wait until your mentoree has finished what he/she is saying completely before speaking – avoid interrupting. Concentrate; you can be tempted to be concerned about what you will say next rather than listening to what is being said. It can be useful to paraphrase what you hear, to check you have concentrated fully.

Sometimes when your mentoree is silent, he or she may be making important discoveries or important decisions. You are wise to evaluate what is happening when silence occurs. Plan not to speak until the other person is ready.

Give God space to move!

An exercise

Get out your diary and make a special appointment with the most important person in your life. The purpose of this appointment is to enable you to spend an hour together just communicating. Plan to give this special person your undivided attention, and to spend at least two-thirds of the time just listening to him or her.

Afterwards, write down how this experience impacted both of you. Be prepared to share about your experience next session.

Evaluation for your mentoree's benefit

Even before the time comes to re-evaluate your mentoring contract with each other, as agreed, check from time to time how the process is going for your mentoree. Be willing to receive criticisms or suggestions and to make other plans if it is not working.

Be aware of things in your mentoree's life that may be affecting how he/she feels about your mentoring relationship. Know when to end the mentoring relationship.

10:

Mentoring example

Here's a typical outline of how a conversation might go when I mentor someone who is looking for help with their preaching:

> Andy: Welcome, great to see you!
> Ed: Thanks.
> Andy: How are you?
> Ed: Pretty good, thanks.
> Andy: Good. We discussed last week that you wanted some help in preaching and we identified that it would be good in the first instance at least to focus upon the preparation side of preaching. Have I remembered that correctly?
> Ed: Yes. I think I need help in other areas but certainly I want to better know how to prepare a sermon. I have kind of got by in the past, but when I was given an unfamiliar passage to preach on last month, I felt a bit at sea and it was then that someone suggested I give you a call.
> Andy: OK. Well as you know I run courses on preaching at CWR, so I have printed off the things I say about preparation on that course. Do you want to take a moment to read that?
> Ed: Thanks.

Ed reads the following material:

1. *Read the text a number of times in the version you will be using.*
Our text or passage may be given to us, or we may have to decide on one

ourselves. There is no rule on how long or short the passage should be. We may use many texts, as in topical preaching.

2. Consult other Bible versions and note any variations.

Use thought for thought (such as the NLT) and word for word (such as the NRSV) translations.

3. As you read, ask questions of the text.

– How does it strike you?

– Is there anything that surprises you?

– Is there anything that puzzles you?

– Are there terms or ideas that are not familiar to you?

– What is the author writing about? What is the author saying about what he or she is writing about?

4. Look for any structure in the text.

Are there repeated words? Are there devices the author uses for emphasis?

5. Summarise the text in your own words.

6. Set the text in the context of the book in which it appears and any obvious wider context within the biblical narrative.

7. Consult Bible study aids.

Although your mind will doubtless start to go to the sermon you are preparing at this stage, try to simply enjoy the process of grappling with the text and meeting God in it for yourself.

8. Ask what is the main idea that is being communicated in the passage.

9. Pray.

Talk to God about the passage, responding to anything you are learning and asking Him for His help to discern its meaning and obey its teaching. How might you need to change your thinking or behaviour as a result of this? What resistance do you sense personally?

Andy: What did you make of the list?

Ed: Yes, really helpful.

Andy: Anything you want me to elaborate on?

Ed: You mention the 'big idea'. What is that?

Andy: Yes, the big idea is something that many preaching experts advocate. The concept of the big idea is that we need to look at what any passage is saying and make sure our sermon focuses on that. Of course, there may be more than one big idea but it's a great discipline to work out what the passage is saying. Once we have the big idea we then look at what we might say in the sermon to help the listener to grasp it in ways appropriate to them.

So if your text for the day was, say, John 3:16, the big idea is that God really does love His world and goes to extraordinary lengths so that we can know Him in this world and the next, and not waste our lives.

A sermon on that verse might focus on whether we think God loves us, exploring in detail how God demonstrates His love, what sending the Son meant, detailing what it means to believe, and precisely what is meant by eternal life. Does that help?

Ed: Yes, I guess I have struggled with wondering what to focus on. This might help.

The conversation might continue with other areas that Ed was concerned with. Please note that I want to tailor my advice to Ed's stage of development. I am giving advice, but he controls what level we work at. When I see what his preparation is like I may find that we have to do some preliminary work on targeted preparation but as a first meeting, I am happy to see what he comes up with and take it from there.

Next steps

You are nearly at the end of this book so it's time to consider what might be next for you. If you have already decided that coaching and mentoring is not something you want to be engaged with, well done for continuing to read till the end. Hopefully you can see the value of the practices and would be open to finding a coach or mentor yourself, should you feel the need.

But supposing that you think that coaching or mentoring, or both, might be part of your future. What next?

Starting out

If your intention is to see whether coaching or mentoring could be become a major part of your ministry or something you will do for a living, but you have little experience, then you could start by offering to coach or mentor family, friends and acquaintances for free. It is probably easier to offer coaching, because you don't need to know their particular world to be of help. But mentoring might work too.

Tell them that you read a book and want to practice. They may believe they are doing you a favour but may come to feel they have done better out of the deal!

It is always better to start small and develop. Don't give up your day job just yet. Set yourself goals of steady progress over time. Coaching and mentoring develops through recommendation and this takes time.

What coaching/mentoring needs do you see in your church, family, friends or work context?

Incorporation

It may be that you have a full-time or part-time role which involves caring for people one to one, as supported full-time staff in a church, as a pastoral carer, in youth or children's work, or in a charity or company.

You may already have ideas on how you can incorporate coaching and mentoring to your role, as a way of helping those you engage with on a daily basis. In some cases it may be appropriate to say that you are coaching or mentoring them. Or it may be best to simply use the coaching and mentoring tools of questioning and listening, without saying you are. This is not to suggest that you are in any way deceptive, just that some people are uncomfortable with the terminology of coaching and mentoring, though at the same time keen to be helped.

Be coached or mentored yourself

You may want the above ideas to become an area in which you are coached or mentored. Find a Christian coach or mentor via a search on the web, or through a mutual acquaintance, and ask them to help you develop your own skills in this area.

Further training

We can only do a limited amount in an introductory book. You may want to enrol on a course. You can check out what courses are available at CWR (**www.cwr.org.uk**) or look at other courses on the web. At the time of writing there is no recognised professional standard for coaching and mentoring. Consequently, there will be many courses offered, both residential and online, that will offer their own certificates of study. At present there is no 'gold standard' certificate that has widespread recognition, but there are some that have a better reputation than others. Be very careful in your research lest you end up paying the earth for a course that doesn't do what it claims.

Further resources

Coaches and mentors use a whole array of additional tools to help them in the coaching and mentoring process. Of particular help are tools that can help them better understand the preferences of the person they are helping.

MBTI

Perhaps the most widely used temperament preference indicator is the Myers Briggs Temperament Indicator (MBTI), though it is far from being the only one of its kind.

> MBTI Step 1 is a personality type assessment that provides an understanding of personal motivations and group interactions. These can be used in a range of ways to appreciate the ways we prefer to live and how these differ from others.

There are four fundamental dimensions of individual difference to create sixteen personality type profiles:

- Extraversion (E) – Introversion (I)
  Where you prefer to get or focus your energy
- Sensing (S) – Intuition (N)
  The kind of information you prefer to gather and trust
- Thinking (T) – Feeling (F)
  The process you prefer to use in coming to decisions
- Judging (J) – Perceiving (P)
  How you prefer to deal with the world around you

The insights gained provide a framework for tackling a wealth of issues that can be applied in both professional and private arenas.

At CWR we run days looking at MBTI, if you are unfamiliar with the approach. Check **www.cwr.org.uk** for the next course. If you are a trained practitioner you might want to take people through the indicator yourself.

SDI

Another test which we have used on courses at CWR is the Strength Deployment Indicator (SDI). The website www.personalstrengthsuk.com says of SDI:

> The SDI is unique because it is a motivational assessment tool as opposed to being a behavioural assessment. The SDI goes below the surface of the behaviours into the motivations and the values that underlie and influence those behaviours. By understanding

what motivates us in our lives to do the things we do, we can better manage our behaviours, and in turn, our relationships with others. Additionally, the SDI integrates going-well and conflict motivations into one easy-to-administer tool that has immediate and lasting results.

Those who complete the test are categorised thus:

Altruistic-Nurturing (Blue): Concern for the protection, growth, and welfare of others.

Assertive-Directing (Red): Concern for task accomplishment and concern for organisation of people, time, money and any other resources to achieve desired results.

Analytic-Autonomizing (Green): Concern for assurance that things have been properly thought out and concern for meaningful order being established and maintained.

Flexible-Cohering (Hub): Concern for flexibility … concern for the welfare of the group … concern for the members of the group and for belonging in the group.

Knowledge of the concerns of the mentoree or coachee will help you know how best to help them. There are useful approaches to how they prefer to lead, manage and deal with conflict.

Transactional Analysis

In talking with people in a coaching and mentoring setting it is useful to be aware that some of the barriers to taking action stem from our upbringing and the emotional drives that still exist within us. In the 1950s Eric Berne developed his theories of Transactional Analysis. He believed that verbal communication, particularly face to face, is at the centre of human social relationships, and developed the idea that we can take on what he called alter ego states: parent, adult and child.

He defined each this way:

Parent

The ingrained voice of authority that we picked up from parents, school teachers and carers who created the rules and provided the boundaries. We can change it, but this is easier said than done.

Child

Berne believed our internal reaction and feelings to external events form the 'child'. He saw this as the seeing, hearing, feeling, and emotional body of data within each of us. For example, when anger or despair dominates reason, the child is in control. Like the parent, we can change it, but it is no easier.

Adult

Berne defined 'adult' as our ability to think and determine action for ourselves, based on received data. This is the means by which we keep our parent and child under control. He argued that if we are to change our parent or child we must do so through our adult.

Transactional Analysis can be summarised as follows:

- Parent is our 'taught' concept of life
- Adult is our 'thought' concept of life
- Child is our 'felt' concept of life

So when we coach and mentor, we are often touching on areas where people may present to us in one of these three states.

Parent behaviour is seen when someone displays physical signs such as anger or impatient body-language and expressions, finger-pointing or patronising gestures. Their language includes words such as 'always', 'never', 'for once and for all', judgmental words, critical words, patronising language and posturing language.

Child behaviour is seen in sad expressions, despair, temper tantrums, whining voice, rolling eyes, shrugging shoulders, teasing, delight, laughter, squirming and giggling. You will hear words such as, 'I wish', 'I dunno', 'I want', 'I'm gonna', 'I don't care', 'oh no', 'not again', 'things never go right for me', 'worst day of my life', 'bigger', 'biggest', 'best', many superlatives and words to impress.

If the coachee or mentoree displays adult behaviour they would be attentive, interested, straightforward, non-threatening and non-threatened. Their language is more measured: 'why', 'what', 'how', 'who', 'where', 'when', 'how much', 'in what way'. They use comparative expressions, reasoned statements, 'true', 'false', 'probably', 'possibly', 'I think', 'I realise', 'I see', 'I believe', 'in my opinion'.

Berne would say there is no general rule as to the effectiveness of any ego state in any given situation (some people get results by being dictatorial (parent to child), or by having temper tantrums, (child to parent), but for a balanced approach to life, adult to adult is generally recommended.

This is of course just a theory, and as Christians we would want to assess any theory in the light of Scripture. But it's useful to observe what is going on, especially if our coachee or mentoree is reacting in ways that we might think are surprising. Our hope and prayer is that the coachee and mentoree grows up into Christ unencumbered by the parental voices or childish tendencies which may impair their development. These tendencies 'interfere' with the coachee's or mentoree's capacity to make progress.

Here is the model in a graphic form:

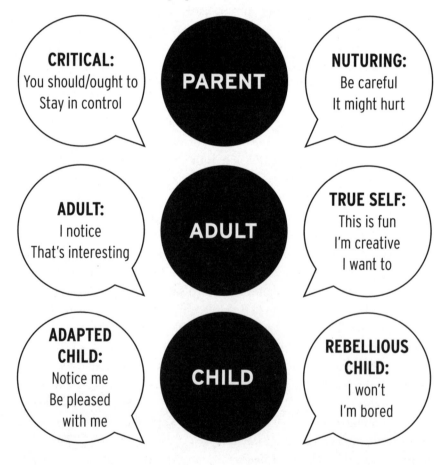

Learning and growth come from engaging the adult with *true self* cooperation.

Questions that minimise interference

These questions are designed to engage both the adult and the true self.

Questions that encourage awareness (getting the clearest possible picture of current reality):

- What is happening?
- What stands out/what do you notice?
- How do you feel about this situation?
- What do you understand about *x*? What don't you understand?
- How would you describe the underlying problem?
- What are the key variables in this situation?
- What is working? What isn't?

Questions that encourage choice (getting the clearest possible picture of the desired future outcome and reminding the coachee that they can choose to move towards it):

- What do you want?
- What would be the cost of not pursuing this goal?
- What would life look like in *x* weeks/months/years from now?
- What changes do you want to make?
- What do you feel most strongly about in this situation?
- Who or what are you doing this for?
- What would success in achieving this goal mean to you?
- What alternatives have you considered?
- Why would you want to do that?

Questions that build trust (in which the coachee gains the greater access to internal and external resources and trusts their ability to move from current reality to the desired future):

- If you could do it any way you wanted, how would you go about achieving this goal?

- What qualities, skills and attributes do you bring to this situation?
- What is the most difficult aspect of this task?
- Where could you find the help you need to accomplish this task?
- How comfortable and confident do you feel about doing this?
- What would it take to make you feel more comfortable?
- What first steps are possible for you?

Adapted from *The Inner Game of Work* by Tim Gallwey.[1]

The questions from each section do not need to be used in any particular order and it is usual to cycle through the different sections in the course of an extended coaching session.

[1] Tim Gallwey, *The Inner Game of Work* (London: Random House, 1999).

Bibliography

You may find the following books helpful. Please be aware that the authors may have a different understanding of coaching and mentoring than is defined in this book.

Tony Stoltzfus *Leadership Coaching* (Tony Stoltzfus, 2006)
Gary Collins *Christian Coaching* (Navpress, 2001)
J Whitmore *Coaching for Performance* (Nicholas Brealey Publishing, 2002)
Andy Peck *Coached by Christ* (eBook) (CWR 2005)
Bryn Hughes *Discipling, Coaching, Mentoring* (Kingsway, 2003)
John Mallison *Mentoring to Develop Disciples and Leaders* (Scripture Union, Australia, 1998)
John C Maxwell *Mentoring 101* (Thomas Nelson, 2008)
Paul Stanley and Robert Clinton *Connecting* (Navpress, 1992)
Howard and William Hendricks *As Iron Sharpens Iron* (Moody Publishers, 1999)

Caring and Counselling

Have you often wondered why people do the things they do and how you could help them change?

Designed for those with an interest in helping others, this is an introduction to the Waverley Framework of Counselling, as taught by CWR. Based on a biblical perspective of what it means to be human and why emotional and spiritual problems arise, this book offers insight into the problems people face and how they can be helped.

The Waverley approach has been proven effective at helping counsellors get to the roots of their clients' problems and address them effectively.

208 page paperback, 172x230mm
ISBN: 978-1-85345-541-4